Spiritual Messages

from

Samuel Smiles

**TIPS FOR
SELF-HELP
IN THE
MODERN AGE**

RYUHO OKAWA

HS PRESS

Copyright © 2020 by Ryuho Okawa
English translation © Happy Science 2020
Original title: *Samuel Smiles Gendai teki Jijoron no Hint*
HS Press is an imprint of IRH Press Co., Ltd.
Tokyo
ISBN 13: 978-1-943869-69-5
ISBN 10: 1-943869-69-3
Cover Image: Engel Ching/Shutterstock.com

Contents

Preface 9

Chapter 1
Spiritual Messages from Samuel Smiles
Tips for Self-Help in the modern age

Introduction:
Happy Science Values Self-Help

Happy Science favors the spirit of self-help	14
I read *Self-Help* over and over again every morning when I had just started working	16
In the world of meritocracy, I tried self-help on myself	19
Happy Science helps purify and master the mind while training the brain	21
Asking questions that come from everyday practice and professional experience	24

Q1 What is "Modern Self-Help"? 26

If the use of machines makes everything like a complete open-book test, then there's a problem 27

Do smartphones and cars contribute to the polishing of the soul overall? 29

Learn what remains universal without being influenced by trends 31

Things to be aware of and what to know when using electronics 33

Q2 Distinguishing the Difference between Self-Help Effort and Self-Centered Effort 37

How to differentiate between self-help effort and self-centered effort 38

Aspiration, continued hard work, and the positive influence you had on others 42

Q3 How to Prevent Yourself from Becoming Satisfied Too Soon 44

Big fish lie in the depth of the water 45

For those who stop making progress when hitting their peak in life 48

A warning to Japan: the self-help spirit in the nation is declining 50

Q4	**What Smiles Thinks about the Thriving Leftist Ideology** 55

Liberal has two meanings 56

Check if the idea strives to make the world a better place 58

Concerns about China's way of development and
the U.K.'s independence 60

How to recognize hypocritical liberal movement 62

Let individuals' motivation become one with the
motivation to develop their nation 63

Q5	**How to Guide People Who Cannot Accept the Self-Help Theory** 68

The greatest results brought about by *Self-Help* 69

"The greatest point about my book is that it creates
many 'unnamed bodhisattvas'" 71

Nurturing more people who "save others" and not who
"need saving" 73

A longer life span means that you can leave behind the
fruits of your efforts in this life 75

Many "unnamed bodhisattvas" will bring prosperity to
nations 77

The Golden Age is not a time of ease but a laborious
time 79

Increasing the number of people who have progressed
through self-help 81

Chapter 2
Spiritual Messages from Samuel Smiles

1 Investigation into the Spiritual Truth of the Church of England

Requesting Smiles's opinion on "Spiritual Messages from Henry VIII" 86

The idea behind self-help is promoting each person to shine 91

The Church of England is a "zombie mansion" in Smiles's eyes 92

Elizabeth I is like Empress Jito, the Japanese nation-building empress 96

2 Churchill is Responsible for the U.K.

"I want some kind of connection with Happy Science, which has similar ideas as mine" 100

"Accomplished men tend to be close by when a queen takes action" 105

Which spirit is currently responsible for the U.K.? 107

What Shakespeare's works taught us 113

The commonalities among Henry VIII, Queen Elizabeth I, Anne Boleyn, and Mary Boleyn 114

3 What Underlies the U.K.'s Prosperity

The connection between the U.K.'s prosperity and
Hermes's prosperity 116

The one who guided Samuel Smiles 119

The Age of Discovery: a time when Christianity
became a world religion 123

The figures in heaven with the same wavelength as
Smiles 127

4 Smiles Succeeded in Generating New Leaders

Interaction with spirits in the heavenly world 132

A time when hardworking people, regardless of social
status, rise above 135

Those who use computers to create utopia and those
who use them as a tool for domination 137

"We transformed this world into a training center to
nurture talent" 140

5 To an Age When People Find Prosperity

Time will choose what will remain 143

It's an interesting age to be alive depending on how you
perceive it 146

From "a king's prosperity" to "people's prosperity" 149

We live in a time of unnamed bodhisattvas 151

Only things that meet the needs of the future will
remain 152

Afterword 155

About the Author 157
What is El Cantare? 158
What is a Spiritual Message? 160
About Happy Science 164
Movies 168
Contact Information 170
Happiness Realization Party 172
Happy Science Academy* 173
Happy Science University 174
About IRH Press 176
Books by Ryuho Okawa 177

Preface

This "Self-Help in the modern age" is a necessity of the times for Japan, as well as for Asian, African, European, and North and South American countries, now.

With a population of about eight billion people, the world stands at a crossroads. As thoughts on social welfare, which have been developing within advanced countries, become an alternative to communism, the whole world is leaning towards the left and becoming red, similar to how the novel coronavirus outbreak that originated in China is spreading across the world map in that same color.

Unless there are more and more people who have advanced through self-help, the population growth on Earth will definitely be blocked by "something" and begin to drop. If more than half of the population in society becomes ill in a spiritual sense, decline will become the only option. If such self-evident truth is no longer understood, that will be the end of a democratic society.

Ryuho Okawa
Master & CEO of Happy Science Group
Feb. 29, 2020

Chapter 1

Spiritual Messages from Samuel Smiles

Tips for Self-Help in the modern age

*Originally recorded in Japanese on January 29, 2020
at Special Lecture Hall, Happy Science, Japan
and later translated into English*

Samuel Smiles (1812 - 1904)

A Scottish writer and doctor. He first began to work as a doctor in Edinburgh, but later became known as a biographer after publishing *The Life of George Stephenson*. His well-known work, *Self-Help*, was published in 1859 and translated into Japanese soon after the Meiji Restoration in Japan by Masanao Nakamura under the title, *Saigoku Risshi Hen*. This Japanese version, as well as *Gakumon no Susume* by Yukichi Fukuzawa, became bestsellers at the time, selling over a million copies and making a great impact on Japan. Other works by Smiles include *Character*, *Thrift*, *Duty*, and *Life and Labour*.

*The opinions of the spirit do not necessarily reflect those of Happy Science Group.
For the mechanism behind spiritual messages, see the end section.*

Introduction: Happy Science Values Self-Help

Happy Science favors the spirit of self-help

RYUHO OKAWA

On the 23rd of this month (January 2020), I already recorded a spiritual message from Smiles (see Chapter Two), but I thought of doing another one, so that we can put this book together.

I understand that a religion that favors self-help is quite strange. The majority of religions say, "Rely on God or Buddha" and so, people normally think, "A religion isn't a religion if it teaches self-help." We are carrying out our activities as we bear this somewhat difficult theme.

In addition, we also have a political party called the Happiness Realization Party (HRP), which is struggling to win. It is because we are a political party of self-help. I'm sure we would get a lot more votes if our party said things like, "By a windfall, cakes and candies will come falling from heaven," instead of advocating self-help. What we say sounds a little strict, so we haven't been able to get the votes. However, without this spirit, I believe the whole country will fall in the future.

Happy Science has published the Japanese translation of Samuel Smiles's *Self-Help* in two volumes (both Tokyo: IRH Press, 2009) [*holds up both books*]. They were translated using modern language by Professor Shoichi Watanabe in his lifetime, along with Ms. Hisako Miyachi.

They were translated using modern language. Yet, the content is still difficult enough that you (Japanese people) would not be able to read the texts smoothly compared to the easier books that are sold in bookstores now. You will find a lot of unfamiliar names and events introduced in detail and it would be difficult to read it without getting stuck. You may have to spend one or two months reading it as you lie around. There is also another version that is a little easier to understand; it's a spiritual message from Samuel Smiles that I published in 2014. The book, *Gendai no Jijoron wo Motomete* (lit. "Seeking the Modern Self-Help Theory" [Tokyo: IRH Press, 2014], only available in Japanese) [*holds up the book*] can be read as a light introductory book.

I read *Self-Help* over and over again
Every morning when I had just started working

RYUHO OKAWA

I have talked about this many times, but I lived in a company dormitory when I was a new employee of a company I joined after graduating from university.

The dormitory in Chiba Prefecture, now owned by Happy Science and called Shifukukan, was my company's accommodation for single people. Happy Science bought this building. I used to live in one of the rooms on the fourth floor of the building.

The bathroom was a shared bathroom, so it used to become crowded when people were getting ready to leave for work in the morning. If I had gone in there with a book, people would see, so I chose a time when no one would come. That was around five in the morning.

What I used to read during that time was a different translation of *Self-Help*. It was translated by Masanao Nakamura published in the Meiji era. The Japanese text was like a translation of classical Chinese text (in the old Japanese literary style) with some footnotes. The book amounted to about 500 pages in total.

I could not read it smoothly, so I remember reading it every day for about 10 minutes, over and over again, as I underlined it in red. This was during my first year at the company.

How did this man who, first thing in the

morning, started out his day by reading *Self-Help* for 10 minutes turn out? Almost 40 years have passed since then, so I think the results can be seen to some extent.

As I read *Self-Help*, I thought, "Let me experiment this with my own life and check if this is true or false," and tested the theories on myself to see what will happen if I continue to follow this exact ethos or mental attitude.

At the time, I had joined a company and became a businessman with a starting salary of a little over ¥120,000, so I was nothing more than a mere new employee. Such a person since then read *Self-Help* many times, went on working with that ethos, and experimented for nearly 40 years. The result is what you see now, so I think there was no lie in what Smiles had said. Even if I had worked in a different work environment, in the end, I would have accumulated a lot, produced results or made achievements, and improved myself.

In the world of meritocracy, I tried self-help on myself

RYUHO OKAWA

I don't mean to sound boastful or proud, but I would also like to mention the following.

Someone who has graduated from the Faculty of Law at the University of Tokyo and has stepped out into society would normally stop studying once they enter university or as soon as they graduate. There are many people like this. Many people would feel like they have done enough after they finish university or once they are on a path to success. Yet, I did not like such attitude, so I dared to keep on studying.

I even avoided joining the kind of companies where people were promoted automatically with age or choosing such kind of path because I disliked that concept. I also disliked the kind of work where people are assured by their qualifications for a lifetime.

Rather, I thought it would be better to choose a path where you cannot succeed without true ability, so I chose a different path from others, a path that others would not want to take.

Trading companies were based on the merit system, so there were many people, even graduates of the University of Tokyo, who were pushed aside into the corners. If you were not efficient with work, then that would mean the end for you.

That is why I dared to join a difficult workplace where educational background had little influence and tested the self-help theory on myself.

This may sound like I am boasting, and people like my son tend to take it that way, so it can be a problem. But my experiment was to test a kind of formula to see what will happen in 40 years when a graduate of the University of Tokyo, Faculty of Law takes on the self-help attitude. What you see now is the result.

I still plan to keep on working a little more, so I would like you to see what happens when 40 years turns to 50 years, then 60 years. Please see it to the end.

Happy Science helps purify and Master the mind while training the brain

RYUHO OKAWA

That is why we have some aspects that are not, in a sense, religious. In religion, there are always aspects that teach about polishing and purifying the mind. On the other hand, Smiles's philosophy-like teachings are about training your brain.

By training your brain, you can work efficiently. This is also great power in modern times. Especially in the world of practical studies, most of its studies cannot be pursued without training your brain.

Spiritual Messages from Samuel Smiles
Tips for Self-Help in the Modern Age

So this is an experiment to see what will happen if we purify and master our mind as we train our brain at the same time. We are doing both. This means that at Happy Science, we are doing both practical work and religious training at the same time.

In this sense, I think our organization is quite unique. It may seem like it is no different from other religions, but there are differences in reality.

At first, we may seem to be taking a detour, but it will be better in the long run. As I mentioned earlier, when a religion only talks about grace from heaven, it is easy to have a good reputation, and there are actually many religions like this. However, I dare continue to preach the importance of studying and making efforts.

For example, I raised five children in my home; I can't help but feel that even though they were raised in the same environment, the stronger the spirit of self-help, the higher in ability and more capable they seem to be now.

On the contrary, the more a person thinks, "I who came down from heaven am great and have talent," like in the doctrine of the divine right of kings, the more a difficult state he or she will be in later on. So, that is why I think the basics of self-help is very important to have.

After all, even if people have differences in ability, they are bound to succeed if they continuously make an effort for a long period. Unless people realize that humans have this potential, democracy cannot be established.

In this sense, Marxism alone is not what destroyed the traditional medieval status society or class society. *Self-Help* had contributed to it and destroyed the class society as well. That's all for the introductory.

Asking questions that come from Everyday practice and professional experience

RYUHO OKAWA

People who listen to and become readers of this book are not truly great figures; they are just ordinary people. So, today, to help you turn into great people-to-be, we would like to ask Smiles questions that come from everyday practice and professional experience to see what he says about the situations of today. Let's get started.

So now, I would like to summon the spirit of Samuel Smiles, who wrote *Self-Help* and had a great influence on Japan since the Meiji Era. We ask that you answer the various questions of the audience.

The spirit of Samuel Smiles, the spirit of Samuel Smiles. Please come down and answer our questions. Thank you very much.

[*About five seconds of silence.*]

Spiritual Messages from Samuel Smiles
Tips for Self-Help in the modern age

SAMUEL SMILES
OK.

Spiritual Messages from Samuel Smiles
Tips for Self-Help in the modern age

Q1

What is "Modern Self-Help"?

QUESTIONER A

Thank you very much for today. *Self-Help*, which you wrote, is still a brilliant classical masterpiece even today.

However, with the passage of time, I think that the environment today has become considerably different from the environment back in your day, especially with the changes in the political system, the spread of smartphones, and the rise of AI. I believe these are the major factors. I would like you to teach those of us who live today what modern self-help is. Thank you.

If the use of machines makes everything Like a complete open-book test, Then there's a problem

SAMUEL SMILES

Machinery is progressing rapidly, so I think that this trend is advancing society in a way that makes things more convenient and takes less effort. This itself, I think, is useful for increasing the value of life or the value of a day.

However, what you must be careful of is that even though such helpful machinery is being developed and sold, the person who can use or possess those things should not start thinking and making efforts in ways that make them corrupted, deteriorated, or lazy in this life, compared to someone who does not have those things.

For example, it may seem meaningless to spend an hour trying to train your brain by solving math problems. There may come a time when children will have access to machines that will give them the answer, but is it really a good thing that they could get the answer by a single push of a button?

Even with languages, I heard about the machines that can translate into multiple languages. Although I am not sure of their accuracy, I heard that they are on the market. I don't know how well they can translate, but what will happen if its accuracy improves and it becomes a futuristic machine that allows you to communicate with 10 or even 20 languages with a push of a button?

I will not object to it if it works as a tool that increases the quality of a person's day, helps make progress in their work, multiplies the wealth of humanity, and brings advantages to the future society. But there is also a possibility that it can deteriorate the ability of an individual in some cases.

To explain this in a little more primitive way, it is like an exam where you can bring your dictionary, hmm... such as an English exam.

If you can bring a dictionary to an exam where you are tested for the meaning of words or idioms or for your translation skills from English to Japanese, then it would be quite easy. Or, if you can bring a calculator to a math exam, it would make it extremely easy.

There may even be cases where you can bring in textbooks, reference books, and other tools, but if we were to head toward making such shortcuts even shorter, then it would be a problem.

Do smartphones and cars contribute to The polishing of the soul overall?

SAMUEL SMILES
Also, there are search functions that allow you to look things up, but if it only works in ways that hinder your ability to study difficult things or things that need perseverance, then it can be a bit dangerous…

For example, as Master Okawa mentioned earlier, it takes a lot of patience to read these two volumes [*holds up both the books*]. You need patience, and they probably contain enough information which makes it impossible to master them by reading it just once.

If, for example, you search "Smiles" or "Self-Help" on your smartphone, you can probably find a number of summaries, and I think it is fine to use them for simple explanations such as this [*points to the materials on the table*].

It will save you time, so there are benefits, but if you're satisfied with just that, you will never reach the level where you can preach or give a lecture on *Self-Help* in public. So, I think it is fine to use it as a guide, but I think that's the extent of how you should use it…

Well, even the spread of cars can essentially cause many people to become weak due to the lack of exercise if they are not careful. Some people experience their body weakening once they start commuting by car, so they may have to train their body in other ways.

What you must try to do is to keep in mind whether or not you are becoming corrupted or losing physical strength, intelligence, will power, and various other things. You must check whether it is eventually contributing to the polishing of your soul or not, while acknowledging its positive aspects or convenience at the same time.

Learn what remains universal
Without being influenced by trends

SAMUEL SMILES

The machinery you are using now would probably all turn into something new and completely different, in say 20 years' time.

In that sense, it is OK to be influenced by trends, but you must, in the back of your mind, always remember what has remained universal and uninfluenced by trends. I mean, there are important philosophies among those that have remained for 2,000 to 3,000 years. These are the things that I would like people to study.

Earlier, Master Okawa mentioned that people usually think that religion is all about relying on God or Buddha, but if we think about Shakyamuni Buddha of Buddhism, I believe he also taught self-help. At the very least, he went through six years of ascetic training and also continued with his training after that.

So, if "self-help" is simply called "training," I cannot imagine Buddhism that doesn't involve any training. Of course, in later years, such a varied form of Buddhism appeared.

However, the teachings of training existed from the beginning, and the fact that he was born into a royal family as a prince probably did not benefit him directly in becoming a religious professional, so he must have abandoned many things. He must have gone through training by abandoning various things one after the other.

He was in a situation where he was able to get anything he wanted, and he had people do everything for him, but he abandoned that and trained in the fields and mountains. So, there was probably self-help of some kind in the beginning and once he reached a certain level, grace came to him as an outside power.

So, I think Buddhism and self-help go well together and that is why they became popular in Japan.

Things to be aware of and what to know When using electronics

SAMUEL SMILES
There are a lot of useful things, but what I'm trying to say is, everything needs to be used in moderation.

For example, just because there is a vacuum cleaner, you should not attach a net and modify it to catch insects and suck up fireflies. There won't be any elegance in the act of catching them. This can happen, so when you look at yourself objectively and find yourself to be like that, then you might want to be a little careful.

Also, there seem to be increasing numbers of people who cannot write kanji (Chinese characters of Japanese words) because of the heavy use of electronic devices. Like so, I think it is important to assess yourself objectively.

Compared to my time, I'm sure it is much easier to write books these days, but in return for this ease, there is definitely something you are losing out on.

In short, the power of the soul isn't likely imbued in a book written in this way, so you should know that.

Some books are even written using cell phones, but they leave no impression, nothing that resonates with the heart or the soul. So, it is OK to use these devices as convenient tools to a certain degree, but not any more than that... If the tool allows you to shorten the time or the labor, then you need to use the time gained for more productive purposes and make an effort to achieve greater results. I believe this will not change in the next 10, 20, or 50 years.

So, as long as you are careful that you do not use these convenient tools in ways that will make you lazy or corrupt, it is OK to incorporate the necessary tools as civilization changes. But if you find that the tools are not helpful, then although you may find it hard to accept, it is important to abandon them.

Many modern people are seeing and hearing the same news over and over again through TV, newspaper, and other media, but some are actually just wasting your time.

So, I hope you will remember that it is important to eliminate things that waste your time, and instead, use that time to concentrate on important matters.

If people become withdrawn and only play games in the house instead of going to work or school, then we will not be able to produce wealth in society. The companies that make the games might increase their sales, but wealth will not be created in the rest of the world.

I would like you to know that there are both the "view of the self" and the "view seen from society as a whole."

Q2

Distinguishing the Difference between Self-Help Effort and Self-Centered Effort

QUESTIONER B

Thank you very much for today. I'd like to ask you a question about self-help effort and self-centered effort.

Hard work in today's day and age is mainly associated with the efforts that are made, for example, in achieving good grades, attaining qualifications, or gaining more skills for work.

In these conditions, along the way, some people can become too self-centered to think of or understand other people's feelings. Some may even stray away from faith because they are so focused on their desires to gain worldly recognition.

I would greatly appreciate it if you could teach us the kind of spirit we should have, so that we can acquire this self-help attitude.

How to differentiate between Self-help effort and self-centered effort

SAMUEL SMILES

From a Western perspective, "the awakening of one's ego" is often thought of as a sign that one has become an adult, so it is not necessarily considered a bad thing. Without this transition, the parents will need to continue caring for their children. Of course, it's important to be independent, but the key here is essentially what they are like on the inside.

I believe that it is important to become an independent adult, have a family, and find a career that lasts your entire life. You must recognize these things as important first.

However, the key here is the content of, or what's behind, the desire to be independent, and whether it is appropriate or not. In other words, the issue is how their independence is received by other people around them.

SPIRITUAL MESSAGES FROM SAMUEL SMILES
TIPS FOR SELF-HELP IN THE MODERN AGE

It is wonderful for someone to study extremely hard to become a doctor with extensive knowledge. Similarly, it is also wonderful for, say, a chef to have plentiful knowledge about their field. Even so, we don't know what their personalities or characters would be like. They could be rude or arrogant like a *tengu* (long-nose goblin). On the other hand, they could be cooperative or have the ability to nurture younger people. So, I think both of these aspects on a whole affect whether one will achieve great success at work or not.

There are people who gain much knowledge in a specialized field and are doing well at work. These people tend to adopt an artisan spirit, where they work alone on a single job. It's quite possible for someone like this to get ahead in their career if they make superhuman efforts. But in a normal situation, these people are usually unable to work with others or nurture subordinates or pupils, and whether they succeed or not will ultimately show in their job evaluation.

In regards to your question—about the difference between self-help effort and self-centered effort, and if they may cause problems if one takes over the other or influences one another—if they are being combined with something different, the results will be reflected accordingly in the achievement of your work and the evaluation by those around you.

In order to study something highly specialized, you would need to study continuously or seclude yourself for a certain period. You may look like a selfish person since you may not be able to fulfill the demands of others at the time. But whether these actions are truly selfish or not should change depending on the work you later produce and the aspirations you have. This period of training is not uncommon for people. Similar to Buddha's six years of extreme asceticism I mentioned earlier, the time spent to awaken oneself tends to appear selfish to some extent. Buddha abandoned his parents, children, and servants to concentrate solely on training, so it may appear like selfishness itself. But it is difficult for a worldly person to judge whether such an act is for selfish reasons or for a grander aspiration to save the entire human race in the early stages.

Let me put it another way. Jesus, for example, his father was a carpenter, so it is likely that he was helping his father's job, I presume... While there is some record of him being a decent carpenter, I do not think that he was making an effort to achieve success in carpentry.

I'd prefer not to believe that Jesus was unskilled, but from his father's perspective, hmm, I think Jesus appeared to have lacked the determination and didn't seem devoted to become a serious carpenter in his youth.

He probably wandered off into the mountains to meditate, study ancient religions, or listen to lectures of other people in his free time. So when viewing him as a carpenter, he may not have been passionate enough. In this sense, as a whole, we cannot be sure of how our lives will be judged until our coffins close.

Aspiration, continued hard work, And the positive influence you had on others

SAMUEL SMILES

Normally, if you work on something for 10 years straight, you cannot go without making progress and becoming distinguished. It would be a little difficult if you happen to have no talent in the field you are in. Say if someone with a phobia of numbers aspires to be a mathematician, it may be difficult for him or her to flourish. But if you have interest and curiosity in the field, and you make a persistent effort for 10 years, the results of your work will show in some ways.

Spiritual Messages from Samuel Smiles
Tips for Self-Help in the Modern Age

The outcome of both what this effort manifests into and the influence it gives to people around you will be evaluated as a whole, so fundamentally, it is up to your aspirations and continued efforts. Effort alone can only take you so far, so in the end, you must think about whether the outcome enriches people's lives in later generations. It is vital to check these three points. So, it is normal to have a period in your life, especially in youth, when you do not know if your efforts are truly self-helping or just self-centered. But it becomes very clear when you assess yourself against the three points: your aspiration, continued efforts, and the influence that its outcome had on others.

It is important to keep this in your mind and know the purpose of why you are making the effort.

Q3

How to Prevent Yourself From Becoming Satisfied Too Soon

QUESTIONER C

Thank you for this precious opportunity today.

This may overlap with the previous question asked, but there are young people in their teens or twenties that tend to expect a return for their efforts and the results they've achieved. They seem to demand a reward that is comparable to the effort they put in. I would be grateful if you could give us some advice on how to prevent yourself from becoming satisfied too soon and how to fight against having too much ambition or desire for fame.

Big fish lie in the depth of the water

SAMUEL SMILES

In the end, I believe this is an issue raised in "Bodhicitta" (an aspiration for enlightenment) of Buddhism. Hmm, whether one can be satisfied with shallow enlightenment is solely dependent on each person's character and their mission in this life.

There are fish that prefer the shallow waters, so we cannot tell them one way is better than the other, but normally, a big fish would not be in the shallows of the ocean. Big fish lie in the depth of the water. You can find them in the depth of the ocean, but not in the shallows of the ocean.

Only small fish can comfortably exist in shallow waters where they could be easily found by people. And all I can say about the people who are satisfied to live where they can easily be seen and caught is that that is the extent of their character.

Spiritual Messages from Samuel Smiles
Tips for Self-Help in the Modern Age

When small fish move in a group, perhaps they are off-guard thinking that the chances of being caught in a net or on a fishing rod are quite low since there are many other similar small fish around. This goes for fish that can group together.

As for big fish, it is more challenging to move in groups. If big fish were moving in a group, it would be quite noticeable. So, they are unlikely to move in schools.

In regards to your question about how not to be satisfied too soon, I think those who are easily satisfied are, likewise, often in the shallow waters with other similarly small fish. They are with a group of other small fish, and just when they realize they are a few centimeters bigger than the other fish, they tend to feel superior. If they are killifish of 10 cm (4 in) in length while others are 3 to 4 cm (1 to 1.5 in), they tend to feel as if they have become a big fish and start to act arrogant because they think they are above the rest.

From a truly big fish, this arrogance and leadership are extremely boring and are nothing more than boastful talk about trivial things.

This may sound simple, but in the end, this will affect the meaning of the person's life and their final judgment of this life, so how far you wish to develop yourself becomes a big factor.

It is like figuring out how deep you need to dig when you are searching for oil, how much effort you need to put in into digging for gold, or how much effort you need to put in into searching for diamonds. If he or she is satisfied with digging a shallow hole, then that will be the extent of them, and that's the kind of evaluation they will receive from people around them.

I don't think any special teaching is required to teach this. The majority of people are satisfied with being in shallow waters. But among them are those who would decide to dive deeper into the ocean only when shallow waters no longer satisfy them. Those who become truly successful emerge from this group of people.

For those who stop making progress
When hitting their peak in life

SAMUEL SMILES

Life is known to be tough and is known to follow the law of cause and effect. For instance, I'm sure there are a number of people who achieved good grades, were told they were distinguished, entered a good school, and landed a good job for having studied hard as a student. But still, there are a significant number of people who have stopped growing and have peaked in life.

So people must be very careful when they find that they are at such a 'peak.' At such a time, whether he or she can think, "This is not my peak," or "I'm in danger if I don't set a goal further in the future," or even, "I cannot stop growing here," is significant.

In order to do so, you should take the lives of great figures from the past as an example and reconsider your life from the eyes of those historical figures, and think, "Compared to them, I still have much to grow."

For example, there are authors who become satisfied as soon as their books start selling to a certain extent and they are able to make a living. And since there are various literary awards in today's age, some who have won such awards may think they have attained success and won fame for themselves. I'm sure there are people who think they are an expert writer for having achieved the Akutagawa Prize, Naoki Prize, or some award and have become satisfied. From my experience, this is very… Hmm. Well, I am not sure if this is appropriate, but when *Self-Help* was translated into Japanese, I was very happy to hear that over one million copies were sold during the Meiji Era and the book influenced Japanese public opinion and the national character to change. In this way, if one writes a book with the hope of leaving a big enough influence to affect a nation's qualities or future to change, then you wouldn't stop there.

A few hundred thousand of my books were also published in England, but there were, of course, times when they were selling and times when sales suddenly dropped. My books stopped selling when the ideas of social welfare of the so-called Communist and Labour Party became prevalent. As the number of people who believed in such a thought grew, the number of people who bought my books declined. This is what led England to enter a period of slow decline in the last 100 years, just as Happy Science has expounded on repeatedly.

A warning to Japan: the self-help spirit In the nation is declining

SAMUEL SMILES
I think *Self-Help* is effective. Yet, even though there are many people in southern China who

uphold ideas with similar qualities as self-help, the so-called 'mentality of China' has a stronger emphasis and tendency toward moneymaking and 'becoming a millionaire overnight.' The sense of spirituality is rather low, so I don't think it is comparable to self-help in a true sense.

The U.S. also shares these characteristics of making as much money as possible. There are people who make not only billions, but tens of billions of dollars.

If the conclusion of self-help is simply to make a lot of money, there is something missing. I think the true meaning of self-help should be balanced with spiritual values.

However, in Japan's case, both are on a decline… Both the spiritual aspects and aspects of worldly success are on a decline, so there is a need for them to make a powerful move to reverse that further.

For example, I doubt that Prime Minister Abe, who has been in office the longest among all prime ministers since the Meiji Era, has read *Self-Help*.

SPIRITUAL MESSAGES FROM SAMUEL SMILES
TIPS FOR SELF-HELP IN THE MODERN AGE

He gives off a quality that is reminiscent of the divine right of kings or *Tensonkorin* (the descent to Earth of Japanese Shinto gods). He seems to be taking advantage of his "hereditary charisma" and using his connections to get himself ahead in society. That is why he appears to be doing well. He has gradually been telling his citizens to take more days off and raise the salary, while he promised to distribute more money to social welfare. He is also saying that the people need not think about retirement or education because the taxes and country will cover both, respectively. I'm sure he hasn't studied the British disease.

The welfare states in Northern Europe may seem legendary or idealistic, but unfortunately, Japan is currently at a turning point of whether it will decline or keep going.

So, even though Happy Science has been sending out various teachings on self-help, the people around aren't listening. The Liberal Democratic Party and opposition parties aren't listening either. It almost seems like these parties are gathering support from people by dragging on the unhappiness from Fukushima and Kobe, and reminding people that in times of emergency, the government will have countermeasures and also look after its citizens in small evacuation shelters. In some ways, this is what lack of religious faith looks like, and it is too worldly in my opinion.

I think it is important for people who have suffered from such disasters to be able to depend on the government for temporary shelter and support. But it is also necessary to understand that it is embarrassing to depend on such help over an extended period of time. One must think of ways to recover quickly or get back on one's feet and find a job that can help them earn enough to pay taxes as a decent human being. If one is unable to think this way, the disaster would have only brought on misfortune and nothing more. Furthermore, if the country begins to use that as a reason for the lack of economic progress, it will only mean that they are just consoling each other for their own failures.

So, I believe there isn't anyone higher up in the Japanese government who has read *Self-Help*. These are the things that concern me.

Q4

What Smiles Thinks about The Thriving Leftist Ideology

QUESTIONER D

While you have just mentioned it a little in the previous question, I'd like to ask you more about self-help from a political point of view. What is called liberal or leftist ideology is thriving very much in Europe and in the U.K., where you, Mr. Smiles, were born. For example, as we saw in the issue with Brexit, one of the reasons why the U.K. wanted to leave the EU is because there was strong opposition against the idea of pursuing a large country or government, like the EU. Even in the U.S., a candidate who strongly advocates wealth tax has come forward in the presidential election, especially from the Democratic Party. If you look around the world, National Socialism or left-leaning liberal ideas or thoughts are expanding worldwide.

In short, as you have just mentioned, the idea of raising taxes would make a country increasingly dependent on social security. Such a way of thinking would take away the freedom of people more and more and the world will head down the path of National Socialism. Now that more than 100 years have passed since the publication of *Self-Help*, I'd appreciate it if you could give us your opinion on this current situation—what we should do and how the world should be? Please tell us any thoughts you may have.

Liberal has two meanings

SAMUEL SMILES

The idea of being liberal is acceptable because this is a thought that allows each person to be independent and, how do I say, encourages each person to be the main character of their life and carve out their own path. But it can also have the opposite meaning where people do not aim for progress. To allow each person to make efforts and succeed, there shouldn't be too many regulations or old hierarchical systems. So in that sense, the idea of being liberal is helping to break down such old systems.

Just like what the person before you had asked, if being liberal leads people to self-centered effort or to have an egotistical nature and makes people care less about one another, then that will only corrupt them. Another meaning of being liberal is when people lose interest in giving back to society or lose interest in developing their society, company, and nation. If this is what society becomes, then people will only start "fighting over limited resources." This is an undesirable state.

So, the idea of being liberal is useful to have when there are too many restraints or too many regulations by which the people are helplessly bound. But if it is used in order to escape from social obligations, responsibility or moral conduct, then the nation will fall and the people will go astray. Being liberal can go in both directions.

Check if the idea strives to Make the world a better place

SAMUEL SMILES
If an advanced welfare state is truly ideal in this world, then that's fine. But the question we should ask them is whether the idea is based on the thought of making the entire Earth or the whole world a better place.

For example, integrated nations like the EU would work if they had a strong passion to save the world from poverty. If they were developing and prospering to save African, Asian, and South American countries from poverty and to decrease such countries' crime levels by making efforts to set a good example as well as to educate them, then such efforts could influence the world positively.

Conversely, if they were trying to protect themselves only by maintaining a system where a fair number of rich people could live an abundant life, it is a matter of time before the number of egoists increases. In other words, the idea of being liberal would be wrong if it only allowed carps to swim inside a pond instead of allowing them to swim freely in a river.

Also, the spirit of mutual support is important to have, but everyone will eventually need to take off. Anything that is running on the runway will eventually need to take off. At that time, it takes courage. So mutual support may help Africa and other countries, but the supporters need to do more than just support and exploit them. The supporters will need to think about how these countries can take off on their own. This is what the supporters should also know.

Concerns about China's way of development And the U.K.'s independence

SAMUEL SMILES

Regarding China's way of development, I am concerned whether they are trying to exploit a foreign country or whether they are trying to set a good example and lead other foreign countries to succeed in the way that they did.

As for whether or not Brexit, the independence movement of the U.K., will succeed, I think it can go either way. I mean, the U.K. will succeed if it regains the spirit of self-help and is able to remake their country into a great leading country through their own decisions, will, and efforts. But the U.K. will gradually isolate itself, decline, and become a small country if its purpose is to simply avoid being taxed extra as a member of the EU and instead use up all their tax money within their own country—in other words, they will fall if their main reason is that they don't want their resources to be taken by the poor members of the EU.

Whether it will succeed or not, every system has its limits. So the bottom line is the leaders' aspiration and what is in their minds. I'm not saying that I disagree with liberals in general. The idea of liberalism should work well against something like a yoke (bondage) or a chain that prevents new leaders from emerging or a new country from growing. So, it really depends on what this idea is aiming for. If liberalism works similarly to how a stampede of tens of thousands of Spanish bullfighting bulls rush through the streets, it will most likely cause tremendous damage.

SPIRITUAL MESSAGES FROM SAMUEL SMILES
TIPS FOR SELF-HELP IN THE MODERN AGE

How to recognize Hypocritical liberal movement

SAMUEL SMILES

Sometimes there are liberals who are hypocritical. In the U.S., especially people in the West Coast, Hollywood, are mostly liberal. These people are actually rich and successful celebrities who are living in large luxurious mansions. They make big money from all the support of and popularity among a large number of common people. So they have a sense of guilt. To escape from this sense of guilt, some of them advocate liberalism showing an antisocial… No, no, no, antinational and anti-government attitude, pretending to be supportive toward the poor.

I won't deny them completely as some of them actually help the poor, which is important. But there are many celebrities who pretend to be liberal because if people find them to be mere celebrities, then their popularity will decline, and they can't maintain their success. So, there are many hypocrites. It is important to be able to distinguish the two.

Let individuals' motivation become one With the motivation to develop their nation

SAMUEL SMILES

Let's take Japan's Sontoku Ninomiya* as an example. It is not easy to tell whether he was a conservative or a liberal. He rebuilt agriculture by reclaiming barren land into cultivated land and turned around bad financial situations of various feudal domains. If we consider what he did as individual efforts, then he will be a liberal, but if his efforts had become systematized and larger in scale, he would have become a non-liberal. In short, the point is whether you perceive the

---

* Sontoku Ninomiya [1787-1856]: a Japanese agricultural leader who helped restore more than 600 villages. He is known for the proverb, *sekisho-idai* ("many smalls make a great"). The author recorded spiritual messages from Sontoku Ninomiya on March 9, 2010.

formula for success as something personal or something organizational.

Parts of the ideology in communism are good, but if a nation tries to manage their country too systematically, or I mean… when a sense of community emerges and people begin to think, "I won't have trouble earning a living since other people are working hard already," such as in kolkhoz, sovkhoz, and the people's commune, what will happen is each person will stop making efforts. This is why about 40 or 50 years ago… yeah, about 40 years ago there wasn't much productivity in China. So the government granted about one-tenth of farms, which officially belonged to the people's commune, to farmers as freely available land. As a result, those parts of the land, in particular, produced a lot of crops, and they were confused about why. Scholars tried to explain the reason in light of the ideals of communism, but they were having difficulty understanding.

The same is said about the current situation in North Korea. The country is poor overall, but when a part of the land was approved as freely available land, that part yielded abundant crops, fruits, and livestock, like chickens and pigs. What this shows is when land is made freely available or properties are approved for private ownership, productivity increases. This is a phenomenon we see.

In the case of the EU, too, if, by more than 20 countries gathering together and forming a community, some member states think that they can survive off of rich countries, then the EU may end up following the same path as communism. A large number of refugees may then flood into the rich member states. Even though the refugees were accepted at first out of generosity, a large number of refugees started to come in, and the problem is becoming serious and giving rise to ethnic conflict.

Spiritual Messages from Samuel Smiles
Tips for Self-Help in the Modern Age

So, what's actually most important is to keep each person's motivation going, and turning individual motivation into a national motivation to keep progressing in a healthy way.

Look at the confusion occurring now in Hong Kong. Hong Kong people are ultimately trying to say that if their region is integrated completely into mainland China, then they will no longer be able to prosper. But the Beijing government cannot understand this. The Beijing government thinks that it is good for Hong Kong to become one with mainland China because they are also succeeding. But the Hong Kong people probably already know that such socialistic success under a planned economy isn't real success. They can see that the system in mainland China won't last because they already have experience succeeding in becoming a world-class financial city. Hong Kong is prospering, not because of Xi Jinping's wisdom, but because of the individuals who worked intensely, gained wisdom, developed their skills in the financial business, and made it to the top. Hong Kong people know what "self-help" means from experience, so that is why there is a clash of values between Hong Kong and China. Political matters such as this are quite difficult and not easy to solve, like cutting through the Gordian knot.

I would like to add, however, that I can agree with liberalism that breaks various restrictions, but if it causes the fall of countries or leads to hypocritical liberalism, then I cannot.

Q5

How to Guide People Who Cannot Accept the Self-Help Theory

QUESTIONER E

Thank you for this precious opportunity today. I would like to ask you about how we could manage both our religious activities and the practices of self-help theory. Today, people in Japan tend to avoid topics on the spirit of self-help. So, when we try to introduce the idea while doing missionary work, we are often met with responses like, "Even if you talk to me about self-help, I can't seem to find the motivation however much I try," or "My current situation won't get any better anyways." There are many people that approach religion with such negative thoughts or feelings of hopelessness and seek to be saved by an outside power, so they cannot seem to accept the idea of self-help. So, I would like to ask, how would you, Mr. Smiles, approach these people and encourage them to change this mindset? I'd be grateful if you could give us some tips on how to guide people in our missionary work.

The greatest results Brought about by *Self-Help*

SAMUEL SMILES

The greatest results brought about by *Self-Help* was that inspired readers began to demonstrate powers they never knew they had. By reading *Self-Help*, ordinary people became capable of not only taking over family businesses, but also attaining much greater success. This wasn't simply because they went to college. It was because they worked hard to realize what they set out to achieve, so the doors started to open. Compared to the parents' generation, the results were far more… well, for example, there was a child born into a family that ran a small inn in a cottage. As the child made efforts and worked hard, the inn eventually grew and turned into a big hotel. There are many more stories like this one and they didn't just happen by chance. It just means that everyone already has the potential to succeed.

Instead of thinking that God created us so that we are no more than our talents, these people believed that God does not think an individual's natural-born talent determines everything. Instead, God thinks that hard work carries more weight than talent and that there are doors that open by working hard.

It is commonly thought that the DNA we are born with decides everything, especially in modern medicine. Yes, DNA can determine our appearance and basic abilities, and humans cannot be horses, nor can horses be dogs. Still, humans have the ability to live their lives in many ways… and to change how they are despite the limits of being human. Recently, more and more women have attained freedom and are succeeding. People can become capable of this once they are free from restraints.

"The greatest point about my book is that It creates many 'unnamed bodhisattvas'"

SAMUEL SMILES

I'd say the greatest point about my book is that it creates many, I believe in your (Happy Science) terms, "unnamed bodhisattvas"*.

Many modern people tend to have certain ideas imprinted in them, such that their family upbringing and natural talent, or their education leading up to 20 years of age determine everything in their life. But as long as you think that "Life is a period of 100 years" as Master Okawa teaches,

---

* Bodhisattvas are people who are making efforts and undergoing spiritual discipline to attain enlightenment all the while trying to save others.

SPIRITUAL MESSAGES FROM SAMUEL SMILES
TIPS FOR SELF-HELP IN THE MODERN AGE

I think you can restart again at any point in your life. You can set off into a new field by acquiring a new ability, knowledge, and experience.

Self-help might sound challenging when you think of it like intensive military training where you are required to, for example, carry 40-kg weights over a mountain. But what the book is trying to say is, "Why don't you try and test out your many possibilities that you already have. The possibilities will blossom after you make a certain level of persistent effort." That is why it lays out many real-life examples to explain to you why you shouldn't give up so easily simply because you think you don't have the talent or skills. So, even for individuals who may seem like the odd one out in their families or may not appear to have praiseworthy talent, through inspiration, they can... You need inspiration first. To make progress, get inspired first, then keep making effort persistently. By making progress you will be able to see things from a new angle, gain new abilities, and carve out a path for yourself.

Nurturing more people who "save others" And not who "need saving"

SAMUEL SMILES

Medicine has been advancing rapidly and so have other fields of study as well. In regards to spirituality, such as religion and morality, however, we may not necessarily be able to say that they are evolving. What we are trying to do is to nurture more people who can save others rather than those who need saving, and this is through demonstrating that people can succeed by being inspired, making continued efforts through the use of small chunks of their time and putting in every spare moment that they have. I believe this is what Happy Science is trying to do as well.

In elections, people commonly vote for the party based on what subsidies will become available, how much pension money they could get, or how much of their medical costs will be covered. People can actually maintain their health into their old age if they proactively make efforts 10 years ahead of time. But these days, much tax money is being used for those who get sick for neglecting their health, and a lot of time is being used to make facilities like hospitals and elderly care homes. As their illness persists for 10, 20 years, these people inevitably affect those around them and drain government funds. To prevent this, people can proactively try to strengthen their bodies, prevent themselves from going senile, and do other various preparations; there are many ways to stay healthy. Many people retire around 60, but for someone who reads *Self-Help*, there will likely be a new path for them. And even if they are past 60, if they continue to walk and train their bodies, for example, it is highly likely for them to stay healthy even at 70.

A longer life span means that you can leave Behind the fruits of your efforts in this life

SAMUEL SMILES

We have no intention of talking about materialism, but the idea opposite of self-help arises if you look at life in this world believing that God or Buddha, or the spirit world does not exist. You might think, "I want quicker results for my efforts because I must be happy while I'm still alive. Those who get quicker results will be happy." This kind of materialistic thinking is quite popular.

Religiously speaking, there is an idea that one who works hard will be rewarded in the afterlife, even if they don't receive recognition in the current life. Christianity teaches something similar to this as well. In addition to this, I think the longer life span nowadays makes it possible to leave behind the fruits of one's efforts in this world to some extent. This is a characteristic of my way of thinking.

Spiritual Messages from Samuel Smiles
Tips for Self-Help in the Modern Age

There are many things to be studied in recent times, so no matter when you begin, you can learn something you would never have learned about in the past. College is no longer limited to those who are 18 to 22 since people can start learning at any age.

So, you should not believe that "where you start from" is all that matters, nor should you wish to be the only ones lazily passing time in an earthly paradise. There are too many people who have forgotten the joy of improving themselves. They think it is suffering. For a long period of time, people desired to be released from the suffering of being pressured to study hard in elementary, middle, and high school and wanted to live a life of ease. But I think the future of Japanese society started to look more uncertain when people started to forget the importance of improving oneself.

I'm sure there are plenty of people who would disagree with this, but in several years, or about 10 to 20 years, these people would be living life without any success, feeling trapped in the dark, or burdening others by depending on their support.

Many "unnamed bodhisattvas" Will bring prosperity to nations

SAMUEL SMILES
I believe something like the story of "the Ant and the Grasshopper" is happening in reality. The story is about how the ant painstakingly collects food throughout the summer in preparation for the winter, while the grasshopper spends its time playing during the abundant season of summer and is met with freezing death in the winter. There is no question that self-help follows the lifestyle of the ant. You may not understand it unless you practice it, but people can improve their abilities and the fruits of their efforts will accumulate. Even when helping

people, if you can help one person, you have the potential to help three, five, or even 10 people. If someone studies very hard and succeeds in building a bridge over a river, that bridge will be useful to many, many people later on. If someone succeeds in digging a tunnel through a mountain, that tunnel alone can help many people by creating an alternative to hiking the mountain. Someone has to take action and play that role.

The work of building a new bridge or creating a new tunnel is great. Even if you don't reap all the benefits of the results, you need to be a person who finds joy in making other people happy. When such "unnamed bodhisattvas" start to emerge, a nation will be ready for the age of prosperity. The reason why a time of prosperity has not returned to Japan since the burst of the economic bubble is that there is a lack of such spirit. This spirit will not be restored through the current government nor by other religions, which often expound on things that are only beneficial in this world. The religious political party which is a part of the administration is probably focusing on making policies that benefit their followers and allow them to scatter money. I believe that if those that don't follow these ways work hard and carve their paths, it will definitely lead to the prosperity of Japan.

The Golden Age is not a time of ease But a laborious time

SAMUEL SMILES
It is said that 2020 is the beginning of the Golden Age, but we must understand it is the start of a truly laborious time rather than a time of ease. We will likely be experiencing the suffering of creation, but we need to encourage the enlightenment movement to change the attitude of the nation as a whole.

SPIRITUAL MESSAGES FROM SAMUEL SMILES
TIPS FOR SELF-HELP IN THE MODERN AGE

Happy Science encountering a wall or an impasse in terms of missionary work means that the enlightenment movement is not making any progress. I'd think the people within Happy Science are limited to their Japanese way of thinking taught to them in school, so they may think that the framework set for them by non-Happy Science people is normal.

However, you have to warn people that once winter comes, everyone will freeze to death. What's important is not to be attracted to things that will give you quick results or things that are within your reach. Instead, it is important to start with the basics and make an effort to carve your path. The hardship you feel now is proof that what you are doing is worth it.

In order for Japan to build a better future, it must redo what was accomplished during the Meiji Restoration. Our hope is that the new era of enlightenment will start in Japan and that Japan will lead the various parts of

Asia, Africa, and South America as their new teacher. I'd also like the declining West to find their spirit once again.

Increasing the number of people Who have progressed through self-help

SAMUEL SMILES
The reality is that without action nothing will change, and with abandonment awaits decline. It seems like a lot of effort is being made to maintaining the current conditions, but perhaps this is because people have not experienced progress through self-help. Please increase the number of people who have experienced this.

On the other hand, miracles sometimes do happen, but Happy Science emphasizes the self-help spirit and is trying to increase the number of people who practice the self-help attitude. I know your organization is trying to increase believers by spreading the Truth that miracles can happen through faith, but by truly understanding the reasons why God created the human souls and trains them on Earth, I want people to realize that creating more awakened people leads to building utopia on earth.

Chapter 2

Spiritual Messages from Samuel Smiles

*Originally recorded in Japanese on January 23, 2020
at Special Lecture Hall, Happy Science, Japan
and later translated into English*

The reason
"Spiritual Messages from Samuel Smiles"
was recorded on January 23, 2020

Five days before this chapter was recorded, the author recorded "Spiritual Messages from Anne Boleyn," "Spiritual Messages from Henry VIII," "Spiritual Messages from Mary Boleyn," and "Spiritual Messages from Elizabeth I" to collect information on the 16th-century English royal family. Each of these spirits spoke on what life was like in England in the 16th century, their current spiritual state, and their past and present lives. Samuel Smiles, a British high spirit, was summoned to gain a deeper understanding of their spiritual messages.

Interviewers from Happy Science[*]

Sakurako Jinmu
Managing Director
Chief Secretary, First Secretarial Division
Religious Affairs Headquarters

Shio Okawa
Aide to Master & CEO

The opinions of the spirit do not necessarily reflect those of Happy Science Group. For the mechanism behind spiritual messages, see the end section.

---

[*] Interviewers are listed in the order that they appear in the transcript.
Their professional titles represent their positions at the time of the interview.

1

Investigation into the Spiritual Truth of The Church of England

Requesting Smiles's opinion on "Spiritual Messages from Henry VIII"

RYUHO OKAWA

Samuel Smiles, Mr. Samuel Smiles, Mr. Samuel Smiles, we've been thinking about this since yesterday, so you'll come, won't you? Mr. Samuel Smiles, Mr. Samuel Smiles, please help us in our spiritual investigation. Mr. Samuel Smiles.

[*About 10 seconds of silence.*]

SAMUEL SMILES

This is Smiles.

JINMU

Hello.

SAMUEL SMILES

Hello.

JINMU

Thank you for your continued support.

SAMUEL SMILES

Yes.

JINMU

We are researching the Church of England…

SAMUEL SMILES

Yes.

JINMU

In "Spiritual Messages from Henry VIII" recorded

SPIRITUAL MESSAGES FROM SAMUEL SMILES
TIPS FOR SELF-HELP IN THE MODERN AGE

on January 18, 2020, it seemed like he has gone to the part of hell that is similar to Abysmal Hell[*] and he is still unaware of his own death...

SAMUEL SMILES
That sounds about right. Yes.

SHIO OKAWA
Do you think this is in line with the Truth?

SAMUEL SMILES
I believe so.

JINMU
Do you happen to know whether Anne Boleyn is currently in heaven or hell?

SAMUEL SMILES
[*Clicks his tongue.*] Well, generally speaking, she's probably in hell, without question.

---

[*] The lowest realm of hell where people who drove many others mad or astray with their mistaken thoughts go. Many are misguided thinkers, religious workers, politicians, and executives. In this hell, spirits are kept in an isolation chamber, so that they cannot negatively influence each other.

SHIO OKAWA

The more I study about her, the darker my impression of her gets.

SAMUEL SMILES

She can't be in heaven shining or glowing.

SHIO OKAWA

Even a monarch cannot get a divorce if he is a Catholic. That just means… If people cannot get

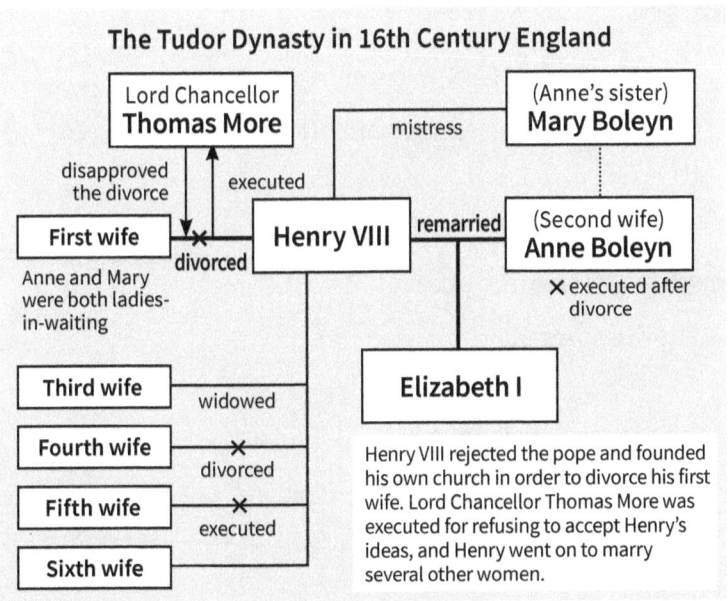

a divorce, hell (in their minds) can expand. So, I feel that it was historically inevitable for a way to break this cycle was found.

SAMUEL SMILES
Henry VIII was a very greedy king, but I think Anne Boleyn was even worse; she was crafty as a fox and incredibly sly.

SHIO OKAWA
Yeah.

SAMUEL SMILES
I agree she was smart, but in a dishonest way.

SHIO OKAWA
She calculated every detail, and made him divorce her…

SAMUEL SMILES
An extremely calculating person.

SHIO OKAWA
She made herself the queen.

SAMUEL SMILES
She loved negotiating her way. Generally speaking, it makes sense for Henry VIII to be (in hell) where he ended up, but in regards to Anne Boleyn returning to heaven... I'm not so sure about that.

The idea behind self-help is promoting Each person to shine

SAMUEL SMILES
So basically, we who are encouraging self-help are trying to say that, "In order to establish democracy, we need self-help." We are promoting each person to shine. Our ideas are conflicting with theirs in the sense that we believe utopia is created, not by the king, but by the people who

make diligent efforts and work hard together as the children of God in pursuit of their ideals.

SHIO OKAWA
Saint Thomas More, who was executed, also mentioned an idea very similar to yours in the recording on January 15, 2020, "Spiritual Messages from Thomas More."

SAMUEL SMILES
Yes, yes. Though, he was someone of higher status. He had status and class.

The Church of England is A "zombie mansion" in Smiles's eyes

SHIO OKAWA
In regards to the Church of England, Ms. Sayaka's book, *Okawa Sayaka no Bungaku no Susume ~Sekai Bungaku hen~* (lit. "Sayaka Okawa's Literary Recommendations ~World

Literature~" [Tokyo: IRH Press, 2016], only available in Japanese) has a section of the research Master Okawa has done for us. We have also asked Princess Diana's spirit too,[*] but it seemed like these spirits weren't saved by the Church of England. Many of them appeared to be asleep under Westminster Abbey…

SAMUEL SMILES
[*Sighs.*]

SHIO OKAWA
How do you view the Church of England?

SAMUEL SMILES
I would say it's a "zombie mansion."

SHIO OKAWA
Hmm.

---

[*] See Ryuho Okawa, *Spiritual Interview with Princess Diana* (Tokyo: HS Press, 2017)

SPIRITUAL MESSAGES FROM SAMUEL SMILES
TIPS FOR SELF-HELP IN THE MODERN AGE

SAMUEL SMILES

I bet there are many people who are unaware of their own deaths and are possessing "mummies."

JINMU

Can't Jesus' light reach them?

SAMUEL SMILES

Hmm. The light may be reaching individuals with faith, but it is hard to say whether the church is truly channeling the light or not.

JINMU

I see.

SHIO OKAWA

When the church was built, do you think it was largely for man-made reasons involving various kings' thoughts over powers?

SAMUEL SMILES

Yes. Oh, but the current withdrawal of the U.K.

from the EU is in a way similar to when the Church of England was established. I suppose the desire for sovereignty is somewhat similar in both cases. They tend to be like this. They dislike being controlled by someone else. It's the island-nation mentality.

JINMU
I see.

SAMUEL SMILES
It might be called the "Viking spirit".

JINMU
So, it's the idea that they don't want to be ruled by the Vatican…

SAMUEL SMILES
Yes, yes, yes. Yes, yes. Exactly. It's tedious to have to get approval every single time. But it is difficult to judge whether this is the same or different from what Xi Jinping is doing now.

SPIRITUAL MESSAGES FROM SAMUEL SMILES
TIPS FOR SELF-HELP IN THE MODERN AGE

Elizabeth I is like Empress Jito, The Japanese nation-building empress

SHIO OKAWA
When Elizabeth I was in power, privateering was authorized and they…

SAMUEL SMILES
Predatory management.

SHIO OKAWA
England has a history where plundering was approved as a way to gain treasures from other countries. And this was England's Golden Age…

SAMUEL SMILES
Yeah, it was the Golden Age. The Golden Age arrived around 1600, but it seems like there was still some overlap with the times of privateering… So there was a definite transition period from being an extremely barbaric country to wanting

to become a modern nation. But I guess they entered the feudal times, right before becoming a modern nation.

JINMU
What kind of person do you think Elizabeth I is?

SAMUEL SMILES
Hmm. [*About five seconds of silence.*] I doubt there are many who believe Elizabeth I went to hell.

SHIO OKAWA
Yes, yes. I agree.

SAMUEL SMILES
Objectively speaking. There are more people who believe that she helped strengthen England to some extent. If I make a comparison in Japanese history… Umm. If we were to name someone like her in Japanese history… hmm. [*About 10 seconds of silence.*] Hmm. Well, I suppose she's

somewhat similar to the nation-building empress. Yes. The person who was involved in compiling the *Kojiki* (Records of Ancient Matters), *Nihon Shoki* (Chronicles of Japan)...

SHIO OKAWA
Empress Jito.

SAMUEL SMILES
Well, I guess someone like her. Thanks to her, the Nara period started to stabilize to some extent. Furthermore, that is also how the current fundamental character of the nation was established.

SHIO OKAWA
England's first slave trade was initiated at the time, and since then, the Age of Discovery began, not just for England, but for Europe as a whole. This is when colonialism began to expand.

SAMUEL SMILES

Hmm. [*About five seconds of silence.*] The British Empire was certainly the leading force behind global development between the 16th and 20th centuries.

2

Churchill is Responsible for the U.K.

"I want some kind of connection
With Happy Science,
Which has similar ideas as mine"

SHIO OKAWA
I'd expect some spiritual powers were assisting the U.K. to thrive.

SAMUEL SMILES
Hmm…

SHIO OKAWA
Are you still in the English Spiritual World right now?

SAMUEL SMILES
Well, I've been here and there. I am approaching

a time when I should start some other activities as well.

SHIO OKAWA
Hmm. Yes.

SAMUEL SMILES
I currently do have some ideas and a plan as well.

SHIO OKAWA
Oh, really?

SAMUEL SMILES
Yes. The teachings of Happy Science are extremely similar to my own ideas, so I'd like to connect with your organization. Don't you agree that our ideas are similar?

SHIO OKAWA
Yes, they are.

JINMU

I agree.

SAMUEL SMILES

Even in this day and age, when talk of social welfare and state socialism are the trend, including in the West, Master Okawa keeps promoting self-help. Although he may have been influenced by Mr. Shoichi Watanabe and others in his youth, the fact that he continues to talk about it now shows how it was a fundamental part of his thought. If this is true, I'd like to believe that the connection with Happy Science was meant to be.

JINMU

Is there a chance you (your soul siblings) are currently already reborn on Earth?

SAMUEL SMILES

Hmm… Actually, well…

SHIO OKAWA
…you're thinking of being reborn?

SAMUEL SMILES
I am considering "coming down" soon.

SHIO OKAWA
I see.

SAMUEL SMILES
I'd be OK with being born soon. Hmm, well I guess it hasn't been that long since I was last born.

SHIO OKAWA
1812 to 1904.

SAMUEL SMILES
Yes. It's only been a hundred years or so. I do feel like now would be a good time to be born again, though.

If Japan heads toward prosperity once again, it will be a good time to go. Though, I'm not sure how I'd feel about it if Japan falls. You want to make Japan prosper again, right? I feel that you want to incorporate the basic idea of modern prosperity in the Japanese people once again. I'm still thinking about it. I do want to make some connections.

SHIO OKAWA
Please do. Especially since there is HSU (Happy Science University) as well.

SAMUEL SMILES
Happy Science's teachings certainly have something that is rather appealing to me. I shouldn't go into too much detail since this recording would become a secret spiritual message about another secret spiritual message.

"Accomplished men tend to be close by When a queen takes action"

JINMU
In regards to the U.K., I think it was at its peak during Queen Victoria's reign. From your perspective, how do you see this?

SAMUEL SMILES
It feels strange to say that the reign of a queen was good. Hmm. Well, I suppose there haven't been many time periods when women were in the spotlight.

SHIO OKAWA
Unusually, there have been relatively many periods in the U.K. when the queen was active.

SAMUEL SMILES
In most cases, there are usually accomplished men who stand close by.

SHIO OKAWA
I see.

SAMUEL SMILES
And they…

SHIO OKAWA
…assist the queen.

SAMUEL SMILES
They all work together to support the queen. When there is an unskilled king or a king with a bad personality on top, they generally all get killed. But when it is a woman, they could get by. The fact that such people served the queen shows how outstanding she was, so it wouldn't be surprising if she had qualities similar to *Amaterasu* (Japanese Sun Goddess). I'm sure such kind of people existed. I don't think this is hell-like at all.

Which spirit is currently Responsible for the U.K.?

SHIO OKAWA
Which god or light of angel is currently keeping watch over England the most...

SAMUEL SMILES
[*Breathes out heavily.*] Watching over the U.K. the most...

SHIO OKAWA
What kind of person might be watching over the U.K.? For example, we are taught that God Thoth[*] is watching over North America.

---

[*] One of the branch spirits of El Cantare, God of the Earth. The great religious master who led the Atlantis civilization to its Golden Age about 12,000 years ago. Thoth is now governing the North American Spirit World. See Ryuho Okawa, *The Laws of the Sun* (New York: IRH Press, 2018) and *The Reason We Are Here: Make Our Powers Together to Realize God's Justice -China Issue, Global Warming, and LGBT-* (Tokyo: HS Press, 2020).

Spiritual Messages from Samuel Smiles
Tips for Self-Help in the Modern Age

SAMUEL SMILES

Ah, yes.

SHIO OKAWA

I know John Lennon and Oscar Wilde both worked in the U.K.* Is Jesus also watching over the U.K.?

SAMUEL SMILES

No, I doubt they are doing much.

JINMU

Or Shakespeare…?

SAMUEL SMILES

No, that's not possible.

JINMU

The time period is…

---

* In the past, the author recorded spiritual messages from John Lennon and Oscar Wilde, who both claimed to be spiritually connected to Jesus. See Ryuho Okawa, *John Lennon's Message from Heaven: On the Spirit of Love and Peace, Music, and the Incredible Secret of His Soul* (Tokyo: HS Press, 2020) and *Spiritual Messages from Oscar Wilde: Love, Beauty, and LGBT* (Tokyo: HS Press, 2019).

SAMUEL SMILES
He's not the type.

SHIO OKAWA
How about Hermes*...?

SAMUEL SMILES
No. I believe Churchill may be responsible right now.

SHIO OKAWA & JINMU
I see.

SAMUEL SMILES
They were on the verge of being destroyed by France... No, not France, Germany.

SHIO OKAWA
Are Churchill, Elizabeth, and Thatcher in a similar spirit world? Or are they in different places?

---
* One of the branch spirits of El Cantare, God of the Earth. He is known as one of the Olympian gods of Greek Mythology, but in truth, he was a real hero of Greece 4,300 years ago. Hermes taught teachings of love and progress, and brought prosperity all over Greece.

SPIRITUAL MESSAGES FROM SAMUEL SMILES
TIPS FOR SELF-HELP IN THE MODERN AGE

SAMUEL SMILES

Hmm. Actually, right now, Churchill…

SHIO OKAWA

So, it's Mr. Churchill.

SAMUEL SMILES

It seems like Churchill is overseeing the U.K. politically. Churchill ranks similarly to Lincoln.

SHIO OKAWA

Oh, really.

SAMUEL SMILES

Yes.

SHIO OKAWA

I suppose so, since his past life was Shakyamuni Buddha's father.*

---

* In the past, the author recorded spiritual messages from Winston Churchill, and in that session, Churchill claimed that he was once born as King Suddhodana (Shakyamuni Buddha's father) in a past life. See Ryuho Okawa, *The New Diplomatic Strategies of Sir Winston Churchill: A Spiritual Interview with the Former Prime Minister Regarding the Age of Perseverance* (Tokyo: HS Press, 2014).

SAMUEL SMILES

Surprisingly, spirits in the ninth dimension don't generally specialize in governing. There are more people who prefer revolutions and reforms, where something new or unknown is about to happen. Many also tend to be people who lay the groundwork, which becomes a clue for later ages.

SHIO OKAWA

There are a lot of them.

SAMUEL SMILES

The people who are currently involved in governing are not such kind of people.

SHIO OKAWA

I see.

SAMUEL SMILES

I guess it hasn't been a hundred years since protecting the U.K. from the Germans, so I think Churchill would still be central to watching over the political activities in England. There are many others who are as powerful. So, my guess is that those powerful people from the 1800s to the 1900s are keeping watch.

There aren't many people from older times, even in the U.K. I'm talking about ancient times.

SHIO OKAWA
Ah, is that right? I guess the history of England started around the Kamakura period of Japanese history.

SAMUEL SMILES
Yes, yes. There were many kings like the ones in Shakespeare's plays, but because they are from such an old time, there is a gap in knowledge. We cannot assume they can provide proper guidance.

What Shakespeare's works taught us

SHIO OKAWA
It seems like Shakespeare has written many plays on the kings of England. Would you say that each of these kings ended up in either heaven or hell?

SAMUEL SMILES
I guess he tried to teach them about…

SHIO OKAWA
…about such things.

SAMUEL SMILES
Yes. So in a way, his plays are equivalent to the Analects of Confucius. I think Shakespeare tried to educate kings by illustrating various fates of kings and proper kingcraft in the plays. It also seems like he pursued to address the issue of love and power a lot.

SHIO OKAWA
I see.

The commonalities among Henry VIII, Queen Elizabeth I, Anne Boleyn, And Mary Boleyn

SAMUEL SMILES
In conclusion, Henry VIII, Queen Elizabeth I, and...

SHIO OKAWA
Anne Boleyn.

SAMUEL SMILES
Anne Boleyn. And, there was one more person, umm...

JINMU & SHIO OKAWA
Mary Boleyn.

SAMUEL SMILES
Oh right, Mary Boleyn.

SHIO OKAWA
Mary Boleyn said in the "Spiritual Messages from Mary Boleyn" recorded on January 18, 2020, that her soul is connected to Mary Magdalene…

SAMUEL SMILES
I wonder if that's true. Hmm… I don't know if Mary Magdalene gave birth to a child (of Jesus's). I'm skeptical that Mary Magdalene would be chosen (by Jesus) to marry…* (Author's note: the conclusion of this spiritual reading is still pending.)

The commonality among these people could be their banishment and setbacks. Surely, these topics could all be in the Shakespearean plays.

---

* In "Spiritual Messages from Mary Magdalene" recorded on January 11, 2020, Mary said she gave birth to Jesus's daughter.

3

What Underlies the U.K.'s Prosperity

The connection between The U.K.'s prosperity and Hermes's prosperity

SHIO OKAWA
Even though they built a new church, it seems like they built it for political reasons involving the way of governance and struggle for power rather than building it out of faith.

SAMUEL SMILES
Hmm. Well, if I daresay so, there was a time way back in the past when Northern Europe, or somewhere around there, was the center of everything.

Although, Hermes's prosperity may have only spanned from the Mediterranean to as far as the Netherlands [*laughs*]. It may not be prosperity brought on by the Vikings either.

SHIO OKAWA

Ah, I see. So, does that mean the prosperity brought on by Hermes is slightly different from the prosperity of Europe after that age of the U.K.?

SAMUEL SMILES

Yes, and there is also the history of the extended battle between the Crusades and Islam, so there's a point of contention there.

SHIO OKAWA

That's true.

SAMUEL SMILES

It's a little hard to believe that the same figure went back and forth between several locations. Yes. Well, it's true that Christianity invaded, but Jesus was no longer Jesus at this point in reality.

SHIO OKAWA

Well, that's true…

SAMUEL SMILES

Yes, Jesus was no longer Jesus.

SHIO OKAWA

Jesus seems to be transformed into this "man-made Jesus" in later generations.

SAMUEL SMILES

Yes. He is sort of like a gate for those who want to pray to God. It's almost like they are praying to God through Jesus because they don't know who God is. And Jesus himself is a "god of the defeated," so I think it is difficult to coexist as a god of prosperity as well. Hmm, well this topic might be beyond me, so it might be best to ask someone else.

The one who guided Samuel Smiles

JINMU

Please speak as much as you like on the following topic. It seems like you contributed to British prosperity as well. Were you receiving spiritual guidance from someone in regards to British prosperity at the time?

SAMUEL SMILES

Let me see… [*About 10 seconds of silence.*] Well, hmm, there wasn't a specific person like me. Hmm… well, hmm. [*About five seconds of silence.*] Well, I daresay I am like the intersection between Buddhism and Christianity. My thoughts lie where Buddhist thought and Christian thought overlap. There weren't many periods like the Industrial Revolution the further you go back in history. Such things didn't exist…

SPIRITUAL MESSAGES FROM SAMUEL SMILES
TIPS FOR SELF-HELP IN THE MODERN AGE

SHIO OKAWA

So, was the inspiration for *Self-Help* from Shakyamuni Buddha…

SAMUEL SMILES

I'd say it's closer to Thoth…

SHIO OKAWA

Wow.

SAMUEL SMILES

If I received any guidance at all.

SHIO OKAWA

I see.

SAMUEL SMILES

I think he gave me some kind of guidance.

SHIO OKAWA
Does this mean that your thoughts overlap with the ideas behind the prosperity in America, too?

SAMUEL SMILES
Yes, yes, yes. The same ideas were spread in America as well.

SHIO OKAWA
Right.

JINMU
I see.

SAMUEL SMILES
Yes. *Self-help* went out of use in the U.K., but picked up the pace in the U.S. next. There was a shift to the U.S. around the time of World War II.

SHIO OKAWA

Did it become the basis for the American Dream?

SAMUEL SMILES

That's right. Japan and the U.S. are now trying to build an alliance, right? I think that's good. Aspects of Thoth and Ra Mu* are beginning to come together as one.

SHIO OKAWA

I see.

SAMUEL SMILES

It's not like there has been an individual like me in recent times. Something like the age of the Industrial Revolution hasn't happened in the last

---

* One of the branch spirits of El Cantare, God of the Earth. He was the great king of an empire that existed on the Mu continent in the Pacific about 17,000 years ago. As a religious and political leader, Ra Mu led the Mu civilization to its Golden Age. Refer to "Openly Recorded Spiritual Message: The Real Thoughts of Ra Mu, the Great King of the Super Ancient Mu Civilization" recorded on February 16, 2018 and *The Laws of the Sun* (New York: IRH Press, 2018).

2,000 years, especially if we exclude the history since the 1700s. So, it wasn't direct (guidance), but Thoth was there as the God of prosperity.

The Age of Discovery: a time When Christianity became a world religion

SAMUEL SMILES
Since Hermes is also the God of prosperity, he had some involvement with the development of churches since he was guiding Jesus. It is unclear if Jesus could have made so much progress on his own. After Jesus had left this world the way he did, it seems like he (Hermes) began getting involved with Islam. Hmm… I guess Hermes is good at business. Things didn't develop quite as much when Jesus was alive.

Hmm. So, in a good way, there were aspects of Hermes's thought incorporated during the Age of Discovery as well.

SPIRITUAL MESSAGES FROM SAMUEL SMILES
TIPS FOR SELF-HELP IN THE MODERN AGE

SHIO OKAWA
Do you mean in terms of trade...

SAMUEL SMILES
In a bad sense, there were reptilian* thoughts involved as well.

SHIO OKAWA
That's right. It does seem like both were involved. Were there both merits, such as prospering, and demerits, like you said?

SAMUEL SMILES
In a sense, Christianity spread across the world through trade, right?

SHIO OKAWA & JINMU
Yes.

---

* The generic term for an alien of reptile-like nature. Reptilians focus heavily on power and strength and are generally very aggressive and invasive. See *UFOs Caught on Camera!: A Spiritual Investigation on Videos and Photos of the Luminous Objects Visiting Earth* (Tokyo: HS Press, 2018).

SAMUEL SMILES
Christianity's success as a world religion has much to do with the Age of Discovery. Without this connection, the religion would have been long gone. I'd think they would have disappeared around the time Islam began. I get the sense that because the Age of Discovery took place in Spain and Portugal, and also in the U.K., Christianity managed to survive and prosper. If this had not taken place, it might have been hard for them to keep going. They might have been completely taken over by Islam. In some ways, the meaning of British prosperity might have been to stop the unipolar domination by Islam.

SHIO OKAWA
Yes.

SAMUEL SMILES
Rome was too close (to the Middle East). If it had been Rome only, the fall of the great

Roman Empire would have led to world domination by Islam. So I sense that British existence was one of the reasons why Christianity did not fail. But of course, there was a core in the East, so there was pressure from there as well, hmm.

Well… Xi Jinping has quite a bad reputation, but without the desire to dominate, nothing would spread, so it's hard to make a judgment on that.

Right now, if there were things spreading from China, it's the Chinese language, Communist ideologies, and Chinese cuisine. That's about it. So, I don't think they are highly advanced. Since culture is being erased, they lack a highly advanced culture. And therefore, they have no "core" in creating a world empire. They are really lacking in that regard. They are about to come face to face with the West, but I don't think they have enough of a core.

The figures in heaven
With the same wavelength as Smiles

SHIO OKAWA

I find that your way of thinking is a little different from Napoleon Hill, but what do you think? I guess you are similar in terms of how you both researched a lot of people and wrote about the keys to success. You also give off a slightly different vibe from that of Yukichi Fukuzawa* or Sontoku Ninomiya...

SAMUEL SMILES

Actually, we are all from the same period. We are from the same age. There were many others like us at the time. They were all interested in personal development. Personal development

---

*Yukichi Fukuzawa [1834-1901]: A Japanese thinker of enlightenment and an educator. The founder of Keio University. Fukuzawa taught the importance of finishing education and of living independently without relying on others. Refer to "'The New Encouragement of Learning' through Yukichi Fukuzawa's Spiritual Messages" recorded on March 3, 2010.

thought originated in modern philosophy. Going back further, I think modern philosophy came from Rome or Greece, which has its origins in what contributed to the prosperity of Egypt and even to Atlantis if we trace it back to older times.

SHIO OKAWA
I see. Were they the kind of people bestowed by God who could share the key points on attaining prosperity?

SAMUEL SMILES
Yes. But I'm not that distinguished. You can mention Samuel Smiles in modern-day England, and no one would know me.

SHIO OKAWA
[*Laughs.*] You mentioned the same thing in your previous spiritual message.

SAMUEL SMILES
Ah, is that so?

SHIO OKAWA
Yes [*laughs*].

SAMUEL SMILES
People would still recognize Yukichi Fukuzawa in Japan, right?

JINMU
Yes.

SHIO OKAWA
I believe so. There is a university founded by him.

SAMUEL SMILES
They may know Yukichi Fukuzawa, but I'm sure there are many others who are no longer known, such as thinkers of that age. That is the extent of our greatness. There are many unnamed bodhisattvas in history. Such kind of people… But I am in tune with someone like Sontoku Ninomiya.

SHIO OKAWA

You meet with him in the Spirit World, don't you?

SAMUEL SMILES

We have a similar wavelength. An extremely similar wavelength. I'd like to think that I am on a similar level as he is.

SHIO OKAWA

I see.

SAMUEL SMILES

It's the basis of prosperity, you know? The basis. Although, we put a bit too much weight on human effort and stray from the practice of simply praying to God.

SHIO OKAWA

But at the foundation of that idea is the belief that each individual is a child of God. By polishing the self and making efforts, one can find the way. Is this correct?

SAMUEL SMILES
If we just prayed to God…

SHIO OKAWA
That's not good enough.

SAMUEL SMILES
The population wouldn't be so… There were maybe one or two billion people just 100 years ago. That was it. But now, there are close to eight billion. Unless people make efforts on their own to increase wealth, they will not attain prosperity.

SPIRITUAL MESSAGES FROM SAMUEL SMILES
TIPS FOR SELF-HELP IN THE MODERN AGE

4

Smiles Succeeded in Generating New Leaders

Interaction with spirits in the heavenly world

SHIO OKAWA

Do you know Mr. Junta Sato*?

SAMUEL SMILES

Well, I know *of* him, but he has the tendency to be a recluse, so he is not the easiest person to interact with. He is not so keen on interacting...

SHIO OKAWA

But you know of him.

---

* A Japanese teacher who taught English. Shoichi Watanabe was one of the students he taught in high school. Watanabe was known as one of Japan's leading conservative speakers. He was inspired by Sato in high school, and this experience became the starting point of his intellectual activities. Watanabe looked up to Sato as his lifelong mentor. The author recorded "Spiritual Messages from Junta Sato" on November 11 and 12, 2017.

SAMUEL SMILES
Yes. I have heard of him.

SHIO OKAWA
I see, I see.

JINMU
Have you met with Mr. Shoichi Watanabe, who has returned to heaven?

SAMUEL SMILES
Ah, ah, ah. I know of him. Benjamin[*] of the U.S.?

SHIO OKAWA
Yes.

---

[*] Benjamin Franklin [1706-1790]: An American politician, diplomat, scientist, and philosopher. One of the Founding Fathers of the U.S. According to spiritual readings by the author, Benjamin Franklin was likely one of the past lives of Shoichi Watanabe.

SPIRITUAL MESSAGES FROM SAMUEL SMILES
TIPS FOR SELF-HELP IN THE MODERN AGE

SAMUEL SMILES

I know Benjamin. Ah, I think he shares similar thoughts.

SHIO OKAWA

I agree.

SAMUEL SMILES

He's my friend, pretty much. So, there are many, maybe dozens, of instigators in various countries.

SHIO OKAWA

There's Hamerton*, too.

SAMUEL SMILES

I'm not too sure about him.

---

* Philip Gilbert Hamerton [1834-1894]: A British thinker, author, and art critic. His well-known book, *The Intellectual Life*, greatly influenced the intelligentsia, mainly in the U.K. The author recorded "Spiritual Messages from Hamerton: Practicing the Intellectual Life in the Modern Age" on October 24, 2018.

SHIO OKAWA
[*Laughs.*]

SAMUEL SMILES
Well… no, no. I don't want to cause any real issues.

SHIO OKAWA
Ah, that's true. Since he (his soul sibling) is currently reborn and living on Earth.

A time when hardworking people, Regardless of social status, rise above

SAMUEL SMILES
Even though kings and monarchs are historically known for making a country prosperous, I tried to challenge this idea by creating an age in which hardworking people rise to success, regardless of social status.

SHIO OKAWA
But this was one way of transitioning, wasn't it?

SAMUEL SMILES
Yes, yes.

SHIO OKAWA
It's not a matter of good or bad. In a world where civilizations rise and fall one after another, this helps different civilizations go through transitions to make humanity evolve, right?

SAMUEL SMILES
Back in the day, people couldn't work unless they were born a king, a chancellor, or maybe as someone who was born into a family of high social status. But nowadays, anyone can start a company and increase jobs that way. In Japan, Ryoma Sakamoto*, Yataro Iwasaki† and those of the like might be the originators. They set

---

* Ryoma Sakamoto [1836-1867]: One of the prominent figures of the Meiji Restoration. He established the first company in Japan, Kameyama Shachu.

up and ran companies. Instead of following boundaries of countries or land, they tried to use companies as an intangible entity that expanded beyond countries and spread across the world.

SHIO OKAWA
Yes.

Those who use computers to create utopia And those who use them as a tool For domination

SHIO OKAWA
In a world where transportation and methods of transcontinental communication are becoming more and more advanced, God must be feeling sad for those who are still bound and limited by their social status or country against their will.

[†] Yataro Iwasaki [1835-1885]: The founder of the Mitsubishi group.

SPIRITUAL MESSAGES FROM SAMUEL SMILES
TIPS FOR SELF-HELP IN THE MODERN AGE

SAMUEL SMILES

So, if Thomas More (is reborn into this world as)...

SHIO OKAWA

Bill Gates.

SAMUEL SMILES

Bill Gates. There would be someone like him aiming to create utopia with the help of computers. But on the other hand, there will be others who use computers as tools to create hell on Earth. Such a battle is happening in different times. In the past, it was a battle between royal authority and papacy... or papal authority, but now the battle involves computers.

SHIO OKAWA

By using computers, there are those who provide people with freedom...

SAMUEL SMILES
Provide wealth…

SHIO OKAWA
There are people who try to offer wealth, while others take advantage of technology as a tool to control people by keeping a close watch on them…

SAMUEL SMILES
That's right. They use it as a tool for domination. These kinds of people always appear. Anything new has both kinds of people.

By the way, a company system contributed to the movement of creating a great country from rivalries between warlords. Through this, people were able to do what only kings could. For example, Ryoma Sakamoto established the navy[*]

---

[*] Kameyama Shachu, a trading company established by Ryoma Sakamoto, was also a private navy.

and Yataro Iwasaki started a trading company, thereby contributing to Japan's development. This is similar to how the U.K. made progress through trade since the Industrial Revolution.

SHIO OKAWA
Meaning, prosperity can happen from bottom up.

SAMUEL SMILES
That's right.

SHIO OKAWA
It's not just prosperity from the top.

"We transformed this world Into a training center to nurture talent"

SAMUEL SMILES
During the time period from what is known as the Meiji Period in Japan, we trained and

produced many competent figures. And we changed this world into a dojo—a training center to nurture talent.

JINMU
I see.

SAMUEL SMILES
We did what is quite difficult to accomplish in the other world, which is to polish and refine human resources by having them "jostle" with each other. We succeeded in producing a large number of new leaders in this world.

SHIO OKAWA
I see. For ordinary people like us, that is something to be thankful for.

SAMUEL SMILES
Japan's success after World War II was much influenced by thoughts from people like Peter

Drucker of the U.S. Having learned about management, Japan found a way to make and expand more companies.

So, things have changed. The things that were once said and done by kings are now being done by thinkers and company heads. And while strong swordsmanship was once valued, preferences are shifting to those who know how to use computers, think of new inventions, or create new products. I'm sure there will be further innovation once we enter the space age.

5

To an Age When People Find Prosperity

Time will choose what will remain

SHIO OKAWA

We are encouraged a lot, just by studying Master Okawa's life. We've been given the opportunity to learn that we can make many people happy with enough hard work and aspiration, even if we were raised in the countryside.

SAMUEL SMILES

If you want to be Santa Claus, you'd have to build a present-making factory somewhere in Scandinavia first [*laughs*]. You will need to gather many materials and do much preparation. If you aspire to make many people prosperous through your "presents," you must first do your own research and prepare diligently. In this current age, an individual can now have great influence. You (Happy Science) have expressed grief about how you aren't expanding enough, but compared to Shakyamuni Buddha and Jesus in their time, I think you have made much more of an impact on the world than you think.

It may be difficult to see these changes when you are living in the moment, especially since there are other similar things. However, the extent of the impact is much clearer when looking at it from the future. Just like how Shakespeare's plays are strikingly different from those of his contemporaries, Mozart's music is also much different from other music, and the music performed by the Beatles is much different from other rock music. In my eyes, I think you are quite popular in this age. There are many other things that are popular right now and it may be difficult to discern the true value of each. But with time, those that should disappear will, and it will be clear what stands the test of time. In this way, time will choose what will remain.

I am not judging Master Okawa for not being successful, being behind schedule, or failing. His way of life is... Well, I think it's impressive to create something world-class even though he was born in a prefecture of the Shikoku region, Japan. In some meaning, he is now trying to make a "worldwide empire" in the dimension of thought. If you can bear a certain number of years, the other competitors will fade away and what remains will grow big, definitely. I think that time is approaching. So, I think you are doing remarkably.

SHIO OKAWA
I understand.

SAMUEL SMILES
And if you could utilize a part of my thoughts, I would be very happy.

SHIO OKAWA
OK. Thank you.

It's an interesting age to be alive
Depending on how you perceive it

SAMUEL SMILES
This discussion about the Church of England has taken a difficult turn. I may not be in a position to pass judgment on a religion.

SHIO OKAWA
I don't mean to say that the Church of England itself is wrong. I'm sure heaven's light is reaching those in the Church of England who have strong faith.

SAMUEL SMILES
Well, the U.K. has a very similar political system as Japan since they still have a constitutional monarchy. So, there should really be somebody with power to rise from below. On top of that, they still have an aristocracy. Unlike Japan, in the U.K.'s case, they have an aristocracy. Don't you traditionally have to be children of

aristocrats to attend schools like Oxford and Cambridge? Traditionally, Japan has more freedom in this regard.

SHIO OKAWA
That's true.

SAMUEL SMILES
Also, they were given a new ground, America, to reclaim. This interesting experiment is still going on.

In China too, the communist party will undoubtedly collapse. Currently, capitalism is spreading mainly in the southern parts of China, and also Taiwan.

I think things will turn out similarly (in China) in the end when many well-renowned businessmen start to emerge. Right now, businesses in China are mostly state-managed, but I think this will eventually change.

They are currently striving toward making money for the sake of money, without the presence of God. But this is not enough. They will eventually need to balance moneymaking with ethics and morals.

I believe the Happy Science teachings to enter China eventually. I'm sure they will. I think you're almost finished with half of your work. I think they will make it into mainland China, in addition to Taiwan and Hong Kong, definitely. The Happy Science teachings will go into China.

SHIO OKAWA
We will do our best.

SAMUEL SMILES
And I think there is still work left with helping the Islamic countries, too. Christianity seems to have significant power, even today. However, as a whole, Westernized countries seem to be weakening, so some kind of innovation is bound to happen. I think this is a very interesting age to be alive depending on how you perceive it.

Being able to reach the world through a video or audio recording captured in one's living space like this is quite a unique situation.

SHIO OKAWA
That's true.

SAMUEL SMILES
Don't you think it's wonderful? I think the current times are much more peaceful and interesting than a world where you have to carve out your own way solely with your skills as a swordsman.

From "a king's prosperity" To "people's prosperity"

SAMUEL SMILES
Well, *Self-Help* is… There really isn't a problem if a king generously helps his people. But it won't last, in most cases. A king is always

a tax levier at the same time. He collects taxes to realize his own prosperity.

Right now, this structure is being adjusted so that it will not be "prosperity for the self," but "prosperity for the people." Yes, that's what I think.

And, Japan should not misunderstand this point.

SHIO OKAWA
If a king has a mentality of increasing the awareness of his people and educating them, then his people could prosper. But what you are saying is that in most cases, with increased power and resources, it is more difficult to be a virtuous king.

SAMUEL SMILES
Yes, well, when one has status, fame, and money, it is difficult to keep working hard. Furthermore, more of them won't understand the concept of self-sacrifice. When people of high status can

no longer understand why it is honorable to try to give themselves up for the sake of saving the world, the royal governing system itself will start to fail. That's how I feel.

Well, for women, it was difficult for them in the past to raise their social position without marrying, but now, different paths are starting to open.

We live in a time of unnamed bodhisattvas

SAMUEL SMILES
We are living in a time of unnamed bodhisattvas. It is starting to become embarrassing to be proud simply because one was a king that lived hundreds, a thousand or two thousand years ago (in a past life). It is embarrassing to base judgment solely on one's birth.

SHIO OKAWA
The times are changing.

SAMUEL SMILES

Yes, that's right. So, I believe periods like the Age of Warring States, the time of samurais, or the time of the merchants happened in order to break this standard. What stops people from always becoming corrupt and decaying is when people exchange positions under a system in which those who work hard rise, while others who neglect their duties fall. In my opinion, it would be good for such a flexible society to expand.

Only things that meet
The needs of the future will remain

SAMUEL SMILES

I'm sure it is very challenging to figure out how to pave the way toward the light in this age of computers and technology. But fundamentally, you must remember that even the things that seem popular now may fade away in 20 years' time. Many of the computer-related companies that are accomplishing much success now could be gone by then. So, I think the only things that will remain are the things that fulfill the needs of the future. There seem to be many companies that only last a single generation. Well… Whether we can create a world of 10 billion people or not is in your hands.

SHIO OKAWA
Thank you very much.

SAMUEL SMILES
Well, this is just the bodhisattvas' law. Please forgive me.

SHIO OKAWA
No problem! There was a lot to be learned from this.

JINMU

Thank you for sharing your vast perspective.

SAMUEL SMILES

Oh, no. I haven't said anything significant. Thoth and Hermes are both great gods. Receiving their guidance would be a great privilege.

SHIO OKAWA

Yes. Thank you.

JINMU

Thank you.

RYUHO OKAWA

[*Claps twice.*]

Afterword

The term, "divine punishment," does not sound very good, but we can see that military conflicts, economic crises, natural disasters, and spread of pneumonia caused by the novel coronavirus seem to have a lot to do with rampant materialism, excessive worship of technology and science, and decline of religion.

With the U.K. as the place of origin, the idea of self-help was developed during the Industrial Revolution or the age of the Great British Empire, when they ruled the seven seas. With the rise of communism and the thought of social welfare, which emerged as a result of the Labour Party within England, the idea of self-help was totally forgotten. It was brought back briefly in Prime Minister Margaret Thatcher's time, but was forgotten once again with the European integration. The world is being disrupted by the leftist liberals who only see social disparity as an issue.

Freedom is always accompanied by efforts, responsibility, and *Noblesse Oblige.* Now that the divine right of kings is no longer valid, there is a need to return to the starting point of democracy.

Ryuho Okawa
Master & CEO of Happy Science Group
Feb. 29, 2020

ABOUT THE AUTHOR

RYUHO OKAWA was born on July 7th 1956, in Tokushima prefecture, Japan. After graduating from the University of Tokyo with a law degree, he joined a Tokyo-based trading house. While working at its New York headquarters, he studied international finance at the Graduate Center of the City University of New York. In 1981, he attained Great Enlightenment and became aware that he is El Cantare with a mission to bring salvation to all of humankind. In 1986 he established Happy Science. It now has members in over 100 countries across the world, with more than 700 local branches and temples as well as 10,000 missionary houses around the world. The total number of lectures has exceeded 3,100 (of which more than 150 are in English) and over 2,600 books (of which more than 500 are Spiritual Interview Series) have been published, many of which are translated into 31 languages. Many of the books, including *The Laws of the Sun* have become best sellers or million sellers. To date, Happy Science has produced 20 movies. The original story and original concept were given by the Executive Producer Ryuho Okawa. Recent movie titles are *The Real Exorcist* (live-action movie to be released in May 2020), *Kiseki to no Deai - Kokoro ni Yorisou 3 -* (lit. "Encounters with Miracles - Heart to Heart 3 -," documentary scheduled to be released in Aug. 2020), and *Twiceborn* (live-action movie to be released in Fall of 2020). He has also composed the lyrics and music of over 100 songs, such as theme songs and featured songs of movies. Moreover, he is the Founder of Happy Science University and Happy Science Academy (Junior and Senior High School), Founder and President of the Happiness Realization Party, Founder and Honorary Headmaster of Happy Science Institute of Government and Management, Founder of IRH Press Co., Ltd., and the Chairperson of New Star Production Co., Ltd. and ARI Production Co., Ltd.

WHAT IS EL CANTARE?

El Cantare means "the Light of the Earth," and is the Supreme God of the Earth who has been guiding humankind since the beginning of Genesis. He is whom Jesus called Father and Muhammad called Allah. Different parts of El Cantare's core consciousness have descended to Earth in the past, once as Alpha and another as Elohim. His branch spirits, such as Shakyamuni Buddha and Hermes, have descended to Earth many times and helped to flourish many civilizations. To unite various religions and to integrate various fields of study in order to build a new civilization on Earth, a part of the core consciousness has descended to Earth as Master Ryuho Okawa.

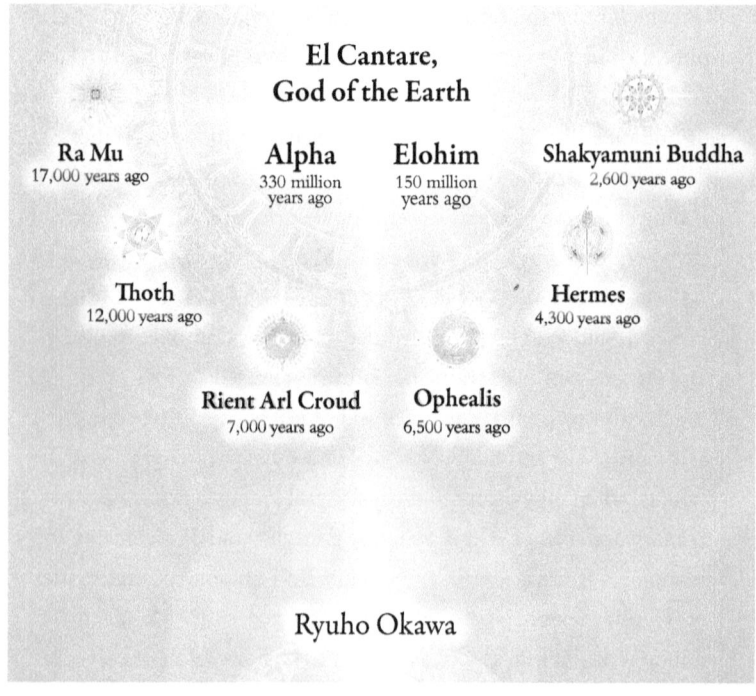

Alpha Alpha is a part of the core consciousness of El Cantare that descended to Earth more than 300 million years ago. Alpha preached Earth's Truths to harmonize and unify Earth-born humans and space people who came from other planets.

Elohim Elohim is the name of El Cantare's core consciousness that lived on Earth 150 million years ago. He taught teachings of wisdom, mainly on the differences of light and darkness, good and evil.

Shakyamuni Buddha Gautama Siddhartha was born as a prince into the Shakya Clan in India around 2,600 years ago. When he was 29 years old, he renounced the world and sought enlightenment. He later attained Great Enlightenment and founded Buddhism.

Hermes In the Greek mythology, Hermes is thought of as one of the 12 Olympian gods, but the spiritual Truth is that he taught the teachings of love and progress around 4,300 years ago that became the origin of the current Western civilization. He is a hero that truly existed.

Ophealis Ophealis was born in Greece around 6,500 years ago and was the leader who took an expedition to as far as Egypt. He is the God of miracles, prosperity, and arts, and is known as Osiris in the Egyptian mythology.

Rient Arl Croud Rient Arl Croud was born as a king of the ancient Incan Empire around 7,000 years ago and taught about the mysteries of the mind. In the heavenly world, he is responsible for the interactions that take place between various planets.

Thoth Thoth was an almighty leader who built the golden age of the Atlantic civilization around 12,000 years ago. In the Egyptian mythology, he is known as God Thoth.

Ra Mu Ra Mu was a leader who built the golden age of the civilization of Mu around 17,000 years ago. As a religious leader and a politician, he ruled by uniting religion and politics.

WHAT IS A SPIRITUAL MESSAGE?

We are all spiritual beings living on this earth. The following is the mechanism behind Master Ryuho Okawa's spiritual messages.

1 You are a spirit

People are born into this world to gain wisdom through various experiences and return to the other world when their lives end. We are all spirits and repeat this cycle in order to refine our souls.

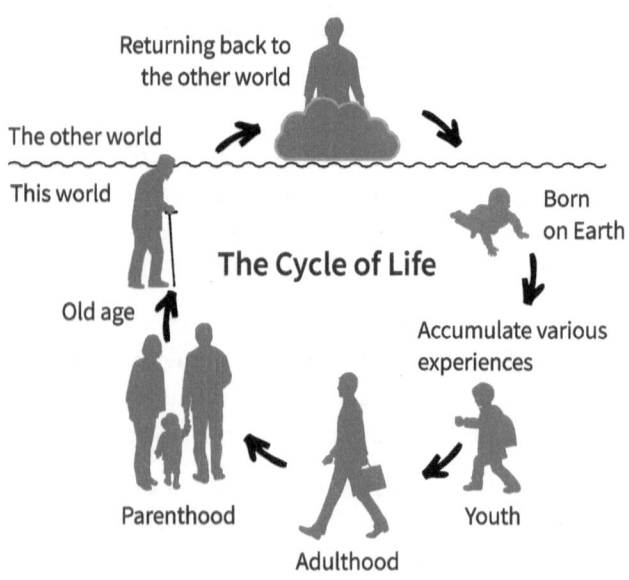

2 You have a guardian spirit

Guardian spirits are those who protect the people who are living on this earth. Each of us has a guardian spirit that watches over us and guides us from the other world. They were us in our past life, and are identical in how we think.

3 How spiritual messages work

Master Ryuho Okawa, through his enlightenment, is capable of summoning any spirit from anywhere in the world, including the spirit world.

Master Okawa's way of receiving spiritual messages is fundamentally different from that of other psychic mediums who undergo trances and are thereby completely taken over by the spirits they are channeling.

Master Okawa's attainment of a high level of enlightenment enables him to retain full control of his consciousness and body throughout the duration of the spiritual message. To allow the spirits to express their own thoughts and personalities freely, however, Master Okawa usually softens the dominancy of his consciousness. This way, he is able to keep his own philosophies out of the way and ensure that the spiritual messages are pure expressions of the spirits he is channeling.

Since guardian spirits think at the same subconscious level as the person living on earth, Master Okawa can summon the spirit and find out what the person on earth is actually thinking. If the person has already returned to the other world, the spirit can give messages to the people living on earth through Master Okawa.

Since 2009, more than 1,000 sessions of spiritual messages have been openly recorded by Master Okawa, and the majority of these have been published. Spiritual messages from the guardian spirits of people living today such as U.S. President Donald Trump, Japanese Prime Minister Shinzo Abe and Chinese President Xi Jinping, as well as spiritual messages sent from the spirit world by Jesus Christ, Muhammad, Thomas Edison, Mother Teresa, Steve Jobs and Nelson Mandela are just a tiny pack of spiritual messages that were published so far.

Domestically, in Japan, these spiritual messages are being read by a wide range of politicians and mass media, and the high-level contents of these books are delivering an impact even more on politics, news and public opinion. In recent years, there have been spiritual messages recorded in English, and English translations are being done on the spiritual messages given in Japanese. These have been published overseas, one after another, and have started to shake the world.

1. The guardian spirit / spirit in the other world...
2. Goes inside Master Okawa in this world
3. Master Okawa speaks the words of the guardian spirit / spirit

*For more about spiritual messages and a complete list of books in the Spiritual Interview Series, visit **okawabooks.com***

ABOUT HAPPY SCIENCE

Happy Science is a global movement that empowers individuals to find purpose and spiritual happiness and to share that happiness with their families, societies, and the world. With more than twelve million members around the world, Happy Science aims to increase awareness of spiritual truths and expand our capacity for love, compassion, and joy so that together we can create the kind of world we all wish to live in.

Activities at Happy Science are based on the Principles of Happiness (Love, Wisdom, Self-Reflection, and Progress). These principles embrace worldwide philosophies and beliefs, transcending boundaries of culture and religions.

> **Love** teaches us to give ourselves freely without expecting anything in return; it encompasses giving, nurturing, and forgiving.
>
> **Wisdom** leads us to the insights of spiritual truths, and opens us to the true meaning of life and the will of God (the universe, the highest power, Buddha).
>
> **Self-Reflection** brings a mindful, nonjudgmental lens to our thoughts and actions to help us find our truest selves—the essence of our souls—and deepen our connection to the highest power. It helps us attain a clean and peaceful mind and leads us to the right life path.

Progress emphasizes the positive, dynamic aspects of our spiritual growth—actions we can take to manifest and spread happiness around the world. It's a path that not only expands our soul growth, but also furthers the collective potential of the world we live in.

PROGRAMS AND EVENTS

The doors of Happy Science are open to all. We offer a variety of programs and events, including self-exploration and self-growth programs, spiritual seminars, meditation and contemplation sessions, study groups, and book events.

Our programs are designed to:
* Deepen your understanding of your purpose and meaning in life
* Improve your relationships and increase your capacity to love unconditionally
* Attain peace of mind, decrease anxiety and stress, and feel positive
* Gain deeper insights and a broader perspective on the world
* Learn how to overcome life's challenges
  ... and much more.

*For more information, visit **happy-science.org**.*

OUR ACTIVITIES

Happy Science does other various activities to provide support for those in need.

- **You Are An Angel! General Incorporated Association**
  Happy Science has a volunteer network in Japan that encourages and supports children with disabilities as well as their parents and guardians.

- **Never Mind School for Truancy**
  At 'Never Mind,' we support students who find it very challenging to attend schools in Japan. We also nurture their self-help spirit and power to rebound against obstacles in life based on Master Okawa's teachings and faith.

- **"Prevention Against Suicide" Campaign since 2003**
  A nationwide campaign to reduce suicides; over 20,000 people commit suicide every year in Japan. "The Suicide Prevention Website-Words of Truth for You-" presents spiritual prescriptions for worries such as depression, lost love, extramarital affairs, bullying and work-related problems, thereby saving many lives.

- **Support for Anti-bullying Campaigns**
  Happy Science provides support for a group of parents and guardians, Network to Protect Children from Bullying, a general incorporated foundation launched in Japan to end bullying, including those that can even be called a criminal offense. So far, the network received more than 5,000 cases and resolved 90% of them.

- **The Golden Age Scholarship**

  This scholarship is granted to students who can contribute greatly and bring a hopeful future to the world.

- **Success No.1**
  Buddha's Truth Afterschool Academy

  Happy Science has over 180 classrooms throughout Japan and in several cities around the world that focus on afterschool education for children. The education focuses on faith and morals in addition to supporting children's school studies.

- **Angel Plan V**

  For children under the age of kindergarten, Happy Science holds classes for nurturing healthy, positive, and creative boys and girls.

- **Future Stars Training Department**

  The Future Stars Training Department was founded within the Happy Science Media Division with the goal of nurturing talented individuals to become successful in the performing arts and entertainment industry.

- **New Star Production Co., Ltd.**
  ARI Production Co., Ltd.

  We have companies to nurture actors and actresses, artists, and vocalists. They are also involved in film production.

DOCUMENTARY MOVIE
HEART TO HEART

In this documentary movie, Happy Science University students visit these NPO activities to discover what salvation truly is, and on the meaning of life, through heart-to-heart interviews.

MOVIES

THE REAL EXORCIST

7 Awards from 3 Countries!

STORY Tokyo —the most mystical city in the world where you find spiritual spots in the most unexpected places. Sayuri works as a part time waitress at a small coffee shop "Extra" where regular customers enjoy the authentic coffee that the owner brews. Meanwhile, Sayuri uses her supernatural powers to help those who are troubled by spiritual phenomena one after another. Through her special consultations, she touches the hearts of the people and helps them by showing the truths of the invisible world.

GOLD REMI AWARD
53rd WorldFest Houston
International Film Festival 2020

BEST FEATURE FILM
17th Angel Film Awards
2020
Monaco International Film Festival

BEST FEATURE FILM
EKO International Film Festival
2020

BEST FEMALE ACTOR
17th Angel Film Awards
2020
Monaco International Film Festival

BEST FEMALE SUPPORTING ACTOR
17th Angel Film Awards
2020
Monaco International Film Festival

BEST SUPPORTING ACTRESS
EKO International Film Festival
2020

BEST VISUAL EFFECTS
17th Angel Film Awards
2020
Monaco International Film Festival

*For more information, visit **www.realexorcistmovie.com***

On VOD NOW
IMMORTAL HERO

37 Awards from 8 Countries!

SPAIN — MADRID INTERNATIONAL FILM FESTIVAL 2019 [BEST DIRECTOR OF A FOREIGN LANGUAGE FEATURE FILM]

USA — INDIE VISIONS FILM FESTIVAL JUL 2019 [WINNER (NARRATIVE FEATURE FILM)]

ITALY — DIAMOND FILM AWARDS JUL 2019 [WINNER (NARRATIVE FEATUREFILM)]

...and more!

For more information, visit www.immortal-hero.com

• Other Happy Science Movies •

1994 **The Terrifying Revelations of Nostradamus**
(live action)

1997 **Love Blows Like the Wind**
(animation)

2000 **The Laws of the Sun**
(animation)

2003 **The Golden Laws**
(animation)

2006 **The Laws of Eternity**
(animation)

2009 **The Rebirth of Buddha**
(animation)

2012 **The Mystical Laws**
(animation)

2015 **The Laws of the Universe - Part 0**
(animation)

2018 **Heart to Heart**
(documentary)

The Laws of the Universe - Part I
(animation)

2019 **The Last White Witch**
(live action)

Life is Beautiful - Heart to Heart 2 -
(documentary)

Immortal Hero
(live action)

- Coming Soon -

2020 **The Real Exorcist**
(live action)

Kiseki to no Deai - Kokoro ni Yorisou 3 -
(lit. Encounters with Miracles - Heart to Heart 3 -)
(documentary)

Twiceborn
(live action)

*Contact your nearest local branch for more information on how to watch HS movies.

CONTACT INFORMATION

Happy Science is a worldwide organization with faith centers around the globe. For a comprehensive list of centers, visit the worldwide directory at ***happy-science.org***. The following are some of the many Happy Science locations:

UNITED STATES AND CANADA

New York
79 Franklin St., New York, NY 10013
Phone: 212-343-7972
Fax: 212-343-7973
Email: ny@happy-science.org
Website: happyscience-na.org

New Jersey
725 River Rd, #102B, Edgewater, NJ 07020
Phone: 201-313-0127
Fax: 201-313-0120
Email: nj@happy-science.org
Website: happyscience-na.org

Florida
5208 8th St., St. Zephyrhills, FL 33542
Phone: 813-715-0000
Fax: 813-715-0010
Email: florida@happy-science.org
Website: happyscience-na.org

Atlanta
1874 Piedmont Ave., NE Suite 360-C
Atlanta, GA 30324
Phone: 404-892-7770
Email: atlanta@happy-science.org
Website: happyscience-na.org

San Francisco
525 Clinton St.
Redwood City, CA 94062
Phone & Fax: 650-363-2777
Email: sf@happy-science.org
Website: happyscience-na.org

Los Angeles
1590 E. Del Mar Blvd., Pasadena, CA 91106
Phone: 626-395-7775
Fax: 626-395-7776
Email: la@happy-science.org
Website: happyscience-na.org

Orange County
10231 Slater Ave., #204
Fountain Valley, CA 92708
Phone: 714-745-1140
Email: oc@happy-science.org
Website: happyscience-na.org

San Diego
7841 Balboa Ave., Suite #202
San Diego, CA 92111
Phone: 619-381-7615
Fax: 626-395-7776
E-mail: sandiego@happy-science.org
Website: happyscience-na.org

Hawaii
Phone: 808-591-9772
Fax: 808-591-9776
Email: hi@happy-science.org
Website: happyscience-na.org

Kauai
3343 Kanakolu Street, Suite 5
Lihue, HI 96766, U.S.A.
Phone: 808-822-7007
Fax: 808-822-6007
Email: kauai-hi@happy-science.org
Website: kauai.happyscience-na.org

Toronto
845 The Queensway
Etobicoke ON M8Z 1N6 Canada
Phone: 1-416-901-3747
Email: toronto@happy-science.org
Website: happy-science.ca

Vancouver
#201-2607 East 49th Avenue
Vancouver, BC, V5S 1J9, Canada
Phone: 1-604-437-7735
Fax: 1-604-437-7764
Email: vancouver@happy-science.org
Website: happy-science.ca

INTERNATIONAL

Tokyo
1-6-7 Togoshi, Shinagawa
Tokyo, 142-0041 Japan
Phone: 81-3-6384-5770
Fax: 81-3-6384-5776
Email: tokyo@happy-science.org
Website: happy-science.org

Seoul
74, Sadang-ro 27-gil,
Dongjak-gu, Seoul, Korea
Phone: 82-2-3478-8777
Fax: 82-2-3478-9777
Email: korea@happy-science.org
Website: happyscience-korea.org

London
3 Margaret St.
London,W1W 8RE United Kingdom
Phone: 44-20-7323-9255
Fax: 44-20-7323-9344
Email: eu@happy-science.org
Website: happyscience-uk.org

Taipei
No. 89, Lane 155, Dunhua N. Road
Songshan District, Taipei City 105, Taiwan
Phone: 886-2-2719-9377
Fax: 886-2-2719-5570
Email: taiwan@happy-science.org
Website: happyscience-tw.org

Sydney
516 Pacific Hwy, Lane Cove North,
NSW 2066, Australia
Phone: 61-2-9411-2877
Fax: 61-2-9411-2822
Email: sydney@happy-science.org

Malaysia
No 22A, Block 2, Jalil Link Jalan Jalil Jaya 2,
Bukit Jalil 57000, Kuala Lumpur, Malaysia
Phone: 60-3-8998-7877
Fax: 60-3-8998-7977
Email: malaysia@happy-science.org
Website: happyscience.org.my

Brazil Headquarters
Rua Domingos de Morais 1154,
Vila Mariana, Sao Paulo SP
CEP 04009-002, Brazil
Phone: 55-11-5088-3800
Fax: 55-11-5088-3806
Email: sp@happy-science.org
Website: happyscience.com.br

Nepal
Kathmandu Metropolitan City Ward
No. 15,
Ring Road, Kimdol,
Sitapaila Kathmandu, Nepal
Phone: 97-714-272931
Email: nepal@happy-science.org

Jundiai
Rua Congo, 447, Jd. Bonfiglioli
Jundiai-CEP, 13207-340
Phone: 55-11-4587-5952
Email: jundiai@happy-science.org

Uganda
Plot 877 Rubaga Road, Kampala
P.O. Box 34130, Kampala, Uganda
Phone: 256-79-3238-002
Email: uganda@happy-science.org
Website: happyscience-uganda.org

 # HAPPINESS REALIZATION PARTY

The Happiness Realization Party (HRP) was founded in May 2009 by Master Ryuho Okawa as part of the Happy Science Group to offer concrete and proactive solutions to the current issues such as military threats from North Korea and China and the long-term economic recession. HRP aims to implement drastic reforms of the Japanese government, thereby bringing peace and prosperity to Japan. To accomplish this, HRP proposes two key policies:

1) Strengthening the national security and the Japan-U.S. alliance, which plays a vital role in the stability of Asia.

2) Improving the Japanese economy by implementing drastic tax cuts, taking monetary easing measures and creating new major industries.

HRP advocates that Japan should offer a model of a religious nation that allows diverse values and beliefs to coexist, and that contributes to global peace.

*For more information, visit **en.hr-party.jp***

HAPPY SCIENCE ACADEMY JUNIOR AND SENIOR HIGH SCHOOL

Happy Science Academy Junior and Senior High School is a boarding school founded with the goal of educating the future leaders of the world who can have a big vision, persevere, and take on new challenges.

Currently, there are two campuses in Japan; the Nasu Main Campus in Tochigi Prefecture, founded in 2010, and the Kansai Campus in Shiga Prefecture, founded in 2013.

Nasu Main Campus

Kansai Campus

HAPPY SCIENCE UNIVERSITY

THE FOUNDING SPIRIT AND THE GOAL OF EDUCATION

Based on the founding philosophy of the university, "Exploration of happiness and the creation of a new civilization," education, research and studies will be provided to help students acquire deep understanding grounded in religious belief and advanced expertise with the objectives of producing "great talents of virtue" who can contribute in a broad-ranging way to serve Japan and the international society.

FACULTIES

Faculty of human happiness

Students in this faculty will pursue liberal arts from various perspectives with a multidisciplinary approach, explore and envision an ideal state of human beings and society.

Faculty of successful management

This faculty aims to realize successful management that helps organizations to create value and wealth for society and to contribute to the happiness and the development of management and employees as well as society as a whole.

Faculty of future creation

Students in this faculty study subjects such as political science, journalism, performing arts and artistic expression, and explore and present new political and cultural models based on truth, goodness and beauty.

Faculty of future industry

This faculty aims to nurture engineers who can resolve various issues facing modern civilization from a technological standpoint and contribute to the creation of new industries of the future.

ABOUT IRH PRESS

IRH Press Co., Ltd., based in Tokyo, was founded in 1987 as a publishing division of Happy Science. IRH Press publishes religious and spiritual books, journals, magazines and also operates broadcast and film production enterprises. For more information, visit *okawabooks.com*.

Follow us on:
Facebook: Okawa Books   **Twitter:** Okawa Books
Goodreads: Ryuho Okawa   **Instagram:** OkawaBooks
Pinterest: Okawa Books

RYUHO OKAWA'S LAWS SERIES

The Laws Series is an annual volume of books that are mainly comprised of Ryuho Okawa's lectures on various topics that highlight principles and guidelines for the activities of Happy Science every year. *The Laws of the Sun*, the first publication of the Laws Series, published in 1987. Since then, all of the Laws Series' titles have ranked in the annual best-selling list for more than two decades, setting sociocultural trends in Japan and around the world.

THE TRILOGY

The first three volumes of the Laws Series, *The Laws of the Sun*, *The Golden Laws*, and *The Nine Dimensions* make a trilogy that completes the basic framework of the teachings of God's Truths. *The Laws of the Sun* discusses the structure of God's Laws, *The Golden Laws* expounds on the doctrine of time, and *The Nine Dimensions* reveals the nature of space.

BOOKS BY RYUHO OKAWA

THE LAWS OF THE SUN
ONE SOURCE, ONE PLANET, ONE PEOPLE

Paperback • 288 pages • $15.95
ISBN: 978-1-942125-43-3

IMAGINE IF YOU COULD ASK GOD why He created this world and what spiritual laws He used to shape us—and everything around us. If we could understand His designs and intentions, we could discover what our goals in life should be and whether our actions move us closer to those goals or farther away.

At a young age, a spiritual calling prompted Ryuho Okawa to outline what he innately understood to be universal truths for all humankind. In *The Laws of the Sun*, Okawa outlines these laws of the universe and provides a road map for living one's life with greater purpose and meaning.

In this powerful book, Ryuho Okawa reveals the transcendent nature of consciousness and the secrets of our multidimensional universe and our place in it. By understanding the different stages of love and following the Buddhist Eightfold Path, he believes we can speed up our eternal process of development. *The Laws of the Sun* shows the way to realize true happiness—a happiness that continues from this world through the other.

The Golden Laws
History through the Eyes of the Eternal Buddha

Paperback • 201 pages • $14.95
ISBN: 978-1-941779-81-1

Throughout history, Great Guiding Spirits of Light have been present on Earth in both the East and the West at crucial points in human history to further our spiritual development. *The Golden Laws* reveals how Divine Plan has been unfolding on Earth, and outlines 5,000 years of the secret history of humankind. Once we understand the true course of history, through the past, the present and into the future, we cannot help but become aware of the significance of our spiritual mission in the present age.

The Nine Dimensions
Unveiling the Laws of Eternity

Paperback • 168 pages • $15.95
ISBN: 978-0-982698-56-3

This book is a window into the mind of our loving God, who designed this world and the vast, wondrous world of our afterlife as a school with many levels through which our souls learn and grow. When the religions and cultures of the world discover the truth of their common spiritual origin, they will be inspired to accept their differences, come together under faith in God, and build an era of harmony and peaceful progress on Earth.

---

*For a complete list of books, visit **okawabooks.com***

The Laws of Steel
Living a Life of Resilience, Confidence and Prosperity

Paperback • 264 pages • $16.95
ISBN: 978-1-942125-65-5

This book is a compilation of six lectures that Ryuho Okawa gave in 2018 and 2019, each containing passionate messages for us to open a brighter future. This powerful and inspiring book will not only show us the ways to achieve true happiness and prosperity, but also the ways to solve many global issues we now face. It presents us with wisdom that is based on a spiritual perspective, and a new design for our future society. Through this book, we can overcome different values and create a peaceful world, thereby ushering in a Golden Age.

The New Resurrection
My Miraculous Story of Overcoming Illness and Death

Hardcover • 224 pages • $19.95
ISBN: 978-1-942125-64-8

The New Resurrection is an autobiographical account of an astonishing miracle experienced by author Ryuho Okawa in 2004. This event was adapted into the feature-length film *Immortal Hero*, released in Japan, the United States and Canada during the Fall of 2019. Today, Okawa lives each day with the readiness to die for the Truth and has dedicated his life to selflessly guide faith seekers towards spiritual development and happiness. The appendix showcases a myriad of accomplishments by Okawa, chronicled after his miraculous resurrection.

---

*For a complete list of books, visit **okawabooks.com***

THE POSSESSION
KNOW THE GHOST CONDITION AND OVERCOME NEGATIVE SPIRITUAL INFLUENCE

Paperback • 114 pages • $14.95
ISBN: 978-1-943869-66-4

Possession is neither an exceptional occurrence nor unscientific superstition; it's a phenomenon, based on spiritual principles, that is still quite common in the modern society. Through this book, you can find the way to change your own mind and free yourself from possession, and the way to exorcise devils by relying on the power of angels and God.

THE REASON WE ARE HERE
MAKE OUR POWERS TOGETHER TO REALIZE GOD'S JUSTICE -CHINA ISSUE, GLOBAL WARMING, AND LGBT-

Paperback • 215 pages • $14.95
ISBN: 978-1-943869-62-6

The Reason We Are Here is a book of thought that is unlike any other: its global perspective, timely opinion on current issues, and spiritual class are unmatched. The main content is the lecture in Toronto, Canada given in October 2019 by Ryuho Okawa.

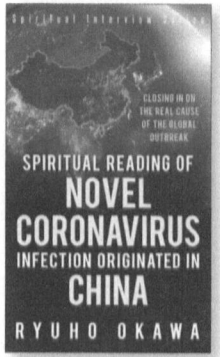

SPIRITUAL READING OF NOVEL CORONAVIRUS INFECTION ORIGINATED IN CHINA
CLOSING IN ON THE REAL CAUSE OF THE GLOBAL OUTBREAK

Paperback • 278 pages • $13.95
ISBN: 978-1-943869-77-0

This worldwide pandemic is not a mere act of nature nor a coincidence, but rather, heaven's warning to humanity, especially China. Through this book, you can find out "the immunity" against the novel coronavirus, among other shocking truths.

---

*For a complete list of books, visit **okawabooks.com***

JOHN LENNON'S MESSAGE FROM HEAVEN
ON THE SPIRIT OF LOVE AND PEACE, MUSIC, AND THE INCREDIBLE SECRET OF HIS SOUL

Paperback • 310 pages • $13.95
ISBN: 978-1-943869-78-7

John Lennon's Message from Heaven is a compilation of his spiritual message held in three separate parts. He speaks his real thoughts and feelings on many topics regarding the world's current and past conditions, and key aspects of the life he lived on Earth.

THE NEW DIPLOMATIC STRATEGIES OF SIR WINSTON CHURCHILL
A SPIRITUAL INTERVIEW WITH THE FORMER PRIME MINISTER REGARDING THE AGE OF PERSEVERANCE

Paperback • 191 pages • $14.95
ISBN: 978-1-937673-80-2

If there is a chance to hear the opinion of Sir Winston Churchill on current international affairs, journalists around the world will probably be interested to hear this. This book made this possible.

SPIRITUAL INTERVIEW WITH PRINCESS DIANA
HER MESSAGES, 20 YEARS AFTER HER DEATH

Paperback • 103 pages • $9.95
ISBN: 978-1-943869-23-7

This spiritual message tells us about the background of the Paris accident and what Diana has been doing since her death. Diana said that through the spiritual conversation, she was able to deepen her understanding on the Spirit World and her own soul, and that she gained the key to return to the world of goddesses in Heaven.

---

*For a complete list of books, visit **okawabooks.com***

THE ROYAL ROAD OF LIFE
Beginning Your Path of Inner Peace, Virtue, and a Life of Purpose

THE LAWS OF GREAT ENLIGHTENMENT
Always Walk with Buddha

I CAN
Discover Your Power Within

HONG KONG REVOLUTION
Spiritual Messages of the Guardian Spirits of Xi Jinping and Agnes Chow Ting

SPIRITUAL MESSAGES FROM OSCAR WILDE
Love, Beauty, and LGBT

THE STARTING POINT OF HAPPINESS
An Inspiring Guide to Positive Living with Faith, Love, and Courage

HEALING FROM WITHIN
Life-Changing Keys to Calm, Spiritual, and Healthy Living

THE UNHAPPINESS SYNDROME
28 Habits of Unhappy People (and How to Change Them)

THINK BIG!
Be Positive and Be Brave to Achieve Your Dreams

---

*For a complete list of books, visit **okawabooks.com***

www.ingramcontent.com/pod-product-compliance
Lightning Source LLC
Chambersburg PA
CBHW020138130526
44591CB00030B/139